The Comfortable In-Between

2024 Poetry Collection

by **Eric Nixon**

Cover image and design by Eric Nixon.

© 2025 by Eric Nixon

ISBN: 978-1-953522-01-6
BISAC: Poetry / American / General

All rights reserved. No part of this book may be copied, reproduced, stored in a retrieval system, or transmitted in any form or by any process without first obtaining written permission from the author; the exception being a reviewer who may quote brief passages with appropriate credit.

That being said, I'm pretty flexible with fully credited adaptations. Please contact me if you are considering adapting or remixing any works contained within this book.

All situations depicted in this book are products of the author's imagination and may not match any reality known to otherwise exist elsewhere.

Published by Double Yolk Press in Lenox, Massachusetts.
EricNixonAuthor@gmail.com
EricNixon.net

MUSICAL PLAYLIST

A few words about the music.

In the notes after most of the poems in this collection is a line telling you about the music I was listening to when I wrote it.

I find that music is not only inspiring, but is intwined with the creative process. In the notes after each poem, I frequently write which song I was listening to when writing that poem. Sometimes the song inspired the poem (almost always the feel of the music and not the lyrics [I honestly don't know the lyrics to most of my favorite songs]), and sometimes the song was just playing in the background. While the song titles often seem like I chose a specific "fitting" song for that particular poem, I would like to say that is never the case. Any song that I happen to be listening to is 100% completely random and dictated by the shuffle feature on my Spotify. I do almost always write to my "Poetry Mix" playlist (at the moment, sitting at about 167 hours of music).

Just like last year, I've compiled every song mentioned in this poetry collection and made a Spotify playlist so you can listen along to the songs that helped inspire my poetry.

https://open.spotify.com/playlist/3wHCOeaCa91NEud0Kjx0IY?si=FkYpjdSzSxaqvsmONfEVmg

I know that link is long and messy, especially for a physical book, sorry!

FORWARD

What's in a title? I don't know. There've been times I've known from fairly early on what I'd call that year's poetry collection – I would write a title of a poem and BOOM, I would be like, "That's it. Right there. The book's title."

This year, however, the title was really elusive. I didn't come up with it until the last minute (December 28!). The other poem titles I had seriously considered naming this collection after were:

What The Cheese Log Tells Me (fun, but too goofy)
Keto For Vengeance (even sillier)
The Scribbled Thrumming (the sorta frontrunner for a while)
All The Nouns Left Behind (eh)
The Eroding Slope (meh)
My Heart Expects It (okay)
Changing My Focus (zzzz)
The Phrase Buffet (intriguing, but not happy with it)
The Comfortable In-Between (yes, thank you)

In a complete contrast, the 2025 collection I'm currently writing, the very second poem of the year is the one I'm 90% sure I'm going to call it. So, we'll see if next year my collection is called *The Hunker Down* or not.

Thank you for reading. I appreciate you.

Eric

TABLE OF CONTENTS

<u>January</u> – 26 poems
A New Me
Christmas Comes Down
What If I Did A Thing
I Can't Look Away
Snow Globe
A Special Order At The Big Box Store
The Things We Used To Hold Dearly
Articles Like This Always Come In Pairs
Fishing For A Job
As We Clean
The Scenery Outside
The Slow Fade To Night
The Skull People
Retaliation
Betterment
Traces
The Essential Elemental Me
Roof Down
The Houses Are Starting To Come Down
A Deluge In The Desert
The Job Of The Dark
The Most Powerful Thing
Watching The Day Pass
Consider A New Path
The Flooding
Interruptions

<u>February</u> – 24 poems
A Level Head Should Have Been In Charge
The City
We Should Watch Bake Off Instead
The Kind Of Opportunity
Anvil Of Consequences
A Lot Early

Lentil Soup
The Idea Is Forming
Dear Universe
What's In the Dock
It Must Be Now
Upturned
A Renewed Flailing
Always The Exception
The Phrase Buffet
Sanding Down Our Edges
Spray Painted Snow
A Mini-Vacation
Outrunning A Minivan
The Exciting Unknown
Did The Unthinkable
The Certainty
A Mind Changed
A Hand Reaching Long

<u>March</u> – 26 poems
Paper Date
Richly Lived Elsewhere
Naming Rights For Disasters
The Collection Of Things
The Words Are The Paints
Ever Since The Line
Building Fences
Scenes Seen
Unable To Comprehend Depth
Gloriously Enchanting
Old Notes
Powerfully Struck
Echoes In The Darkness
The Thermometer Is The One Who Calls It
By My Side
Spend More Time
The Generically Named
The Collective Wheel

Tuning Fork
The Ambiance Plays A Role
Small Potatoes
Orange Cat Tail On My Keyboard
Returning The Favor
The High Holy Day
Something Found
Distant Squirrel

<u>April</u> – 12 poems
Spring Is Sneaky
Polite Dryer
Will AI Replace Me
The Echoing Edge
What May Land On The Paper
Like The Page
Going To Be Great
I Think It Was The Cucumber
Did The Math
At The Click
Demanding Attention
Fifty

<u>May</u> – 20 poems
Spring Is Blooming
Seventeen Years
The Interrupters
Ghost Ticks
The Act Of Stumbling
Fade And Fall
Solely And Only
Bundled-Up Notions
Resonance
If Not, Then Oops
Sparking
They Want
With Each Application

A Portland Song
What The Cheese Log Tells Me
Past The Here
No Sign of Sine
You Can't Coddle
Keto For Vengeance
Distill And Define

<u>June</u> – 26 poems
Punk Shoe Wool
The Scribbled Thrumming
Why Is My Neighbor Mowing Completely Naked
The Touch Removed
The Reason To Loop Back
The Breadcrumbs Of Existence
Static Cling
Gentle Rain
The Approaching Thunder
The Creative Inside
Scam Texts
Perpetual Motion Machine
This Is Where I Am
Getting Started
Equaling This Place
She Knows It All
Grilling View
A Stunning Inundation
Solstice Waning
Survey Worried
The Hero
The Arid Landscape
Regret
The Brave Faithful
Suddenly Became Popular Somehow
Doing Double Duty

July – 16 poems
Sporadic Explosions
I Started Something New
Feel The Pull
A New Phase Of Me
I Simply Won't
The Sun Will Still Rise
A Rancid Patchouli Way
And Naturally, Expansion
Something Sustainable
The Sparkle Of Fireflies
Was Anything Really Missed?
The Perfect Response
While The Eyes
Brevity
Bananas
Wary Of The Bear

August – 10 poems
The Bottle Of You
Click Click
Rudderless
All The Nouns Left Behind
Directions
A Fresh Resetting
Stripped Of His Soapbox Moment
Pop Ups
The Position
Reset Refocus Regroup

September – 20 poems
Stickers
The Best Summer Ever
The Routine Of Creation
Struttin' Their Puffy Stuffs
The Nights Too Cool
I Hit An Age

In The Waiting Room
Within Reach
Lifting Up
Steadfastly Refusing To Comply
A Grinning Sideways Smile
It Still Feels Too Early
Notably Apart
The Eroding Slope
The Act Of Creation
Reinterpreted Beauty
When The Lightning Flows
Emotional Paint
Knowing When To Write
An Attempt To Sway The Business

<u>October</u> – 24 poems
Portobello Road
A Worst Class Experience
Separated By The Ha-Ha
Bath
A Repurposing
English Country Roads
Fleece Alley
Model Village
What Does Matter
Seen The Aurora
Scooch
Nothing But A Folly
Driving On The Left
Back To London
Walking Around Mayfair
The Best Way To Move
Portraiture As The Focus
Dance Booth G
I Am The Champion
I Knew A Guy
The Tube
Just A Quiet Space

The Speedboat Tour
Royal Warrant

<u>November</u> – 26 poems
A Dudebro Chad
A Tornado Of Color
Missing The Culture
A Portrait Faded
Hunker Mode
A Knowledge Of History
The End Result
Bullies Emboldened
The Dark Cloud
Maybe I Am In Control
The Smoothing Folds
I Might Need Another Month
At These Latitudes
The Fruitless Effort
An Apology To The Birds
Play It Endlessly On Repeat
A Pretty Great Idea
Fran Lebowitz
The Lunch Void
Not Enough To Stop
Splitting Hairs
Absorb It All
The New Annual Norm
Yet Another
High Art
I Have No Choice But To Risk It

<u>December</u> – 57 poems
The Lightest Glaze
The Stark Line
Coincidence
Nothing Gets In The Way Of Profit
Insulating

The Light Fluffy Snow
Lighting The Way
Four Tarot Cards
Weekend Ahead
Chilly Stick Season
While The Countries
Sometimes The Weight
Dark Day
Drop Splashing
Doing The Best He Can
Listening To What The Rain Was Saying
Late To Start
The Wondering
Writer's Block
Errant Flakes
Fight Or Flight
Anger At The Buffet
Trust The Intuition
Verbal Voyaging
We Spend Both
From Back In Simpler Times
Born This Week
A Degree
Speedbumping
Tightrope Walking
Vivid Remembrance
Too Warm For December
A Welcome Postcard
With The Eagles Of My Future Self
So Few Seconds
My Heart Expects It
Unaware Of The Options
Manufactured Escape
The Beats
The Damage Will Be Done
Delft
Watching Out The Window
The Patterns Of The Clouds
People Are Forgotten

Doubly Determined
A Casualty
The Day After The Exchange Of Power
The Cultural Season
The Snow Is Here
Productivity Has Melted
The Near Vicinity
The Ideas Never Stop
Impossibly Stacked
Threaten Greenland
Changing My Focus
The Comfortable In-Between
Only A Few Hours Left

2024 total: 287

JANUARY

A New Me

Today is
The first
A new year
A new me
If you pretend
That the other years
Leading up to now
Don't count
For anything
But they do
You can't ignore
What you've
Been through
That would be
Irresponsible,
Foolhardy,
And a little bit
Reckless
To wish away
The past self.
Sure, work to change
That's great,
Strive to be different
Improve continuously
But don't pretend
The drive to this point
Never happened
Because it did
And it made you
Who you are

January 1, 2024
Lenox, Massachusetts

Written while listening to "Soft Stud" by Black Belt Eagle Scout.

January

Christmas Comes Down

Stopping downtown today
Seeing a town worker
Unwinding strings of lights
And garland from the sign
In front of the library
Piling at his feet
To be put back in storage
For another ten months
Struck a chord with me
Giving inspiration
To do the same thing
When I got home
Apparently,
Today's the day when
Christmas comes down
And we all move on
With the fresh year
And the impending winter

        January 3, 2024
        Lenox, Massachusetts

True story.

Written while listening to "We Lost Everything" by The Dears.

What If I Did A Thing

What if I did a thing
Where I did one thing
Each and every day
Steadily, consistently,
For the entirety of the year?
I guess I'd have a lot
Of that one thing
But the thing is
I don't know what yet
Maybe I'll write a poem
Every day, day after day,
And have a massive collection
To publish next year –
The biggest one yet;
Or, maybe I'll take
A photograph a day
And have a neat photo album
Or art. I could make art.
What I'm getting at
Is if you tried this
You could have done
A whole bunch of something
Enough to make a book,
An album, a record,
A *something* that you could
Look at next year
And feel proud of yourself
For having done the *thing*
And, who knows,
It could inspire you
To keep it up
Year after year
Cementing you
As an expert
As an authority
In the thing you do

January

January 3, 2024
Lenox, Massachusetts

Written while listening to "Ready, Able" by Grizzly Bear.

What if you did this? What would you do?

I Can't Look Away

I can't look away
At the impending thing
That's about to happen
Despite knowing
Full well
What the equation
Consists of:
That this plus that
Equals the thing
The inevitable outcome
That always occurs
And, instead of acting
In a rational way
Vaguely resembling
Self-preservation
I stare, wide-eyed,
Mouth agape,
As if I were someone
Who truly had no idea
The danger
I was in for

              January 3, 2024
              Lenox, Massachusetts

Written while listening to "Cake By The Ocean" by DNCE.

January

Snow Globe

The faint snow
Squalling around
Like living in a
Real-life snow globe
Was not predicted
But was still
Greatly appreciated

        January 4, 2024
        Lenox, Massachusetts

We have a "big" snowstorm coming this weekend (only six to eight inches, but it'll be the most snow we've gotten in a couple of years), but nothing was predicted for today…but we ended up getting a surprisingly thick snow squall of huge flakes slowly falling. Then, the wind whipped up and really made everything look white. The snow didn't last, as it melted immediately, but it was still very neat to see.

Written while listening to "Dead American Writers" by Tired Pony.

A Special Order At The Big Box Store

The awkwardly odd man
Wanted to place
A special order
At the big box store
And was told
They didn't do that
They couldn't get him
The larger size bag
Of "Fun Sized" chocolates
With the certain percentage
Of dark chocolate
That he really needed
Which flustered him
As he tightly gripped
His worn bike helmet
While explaining
Why what he wanted
Was healthier
And they should carry it
In the larger size
That may or may not
Even be something
That's made at all
The employees responded
By shrugging and saying
They don't order anything
It all comes from "corporate"
What they want them to sell
Just shows up on a truck
And that's that
The man really didn't like this
But still bought some chocolate
In the smaller sized bag
He didn't want
And made sure
To show his displeasure
By leaving his empty cart

January

Right in front of the exit
In the way of others
Trying to leave
With their purchases
Who didn't even notice
They just walked around it
Until a cart cowboy
Saw it and corralled it
Putting it in its proper place
And the world
Could finally continue

        January 4, 2024
        Lenox, Massachusetts

This happened yesterday at Target. It seems like a brief encounter from this poem, but it actually took like fifteen minutes, and I was stuck behind him trying to pick up my online order.

Written while listening to "I Bet It Stung" by Tegan and Sara.

The Comfortable In-Between

The Things We Used To Hold Dearly

The things we used to hold
Dearly
When we were young and
Silly
Liking something because
It was absurd and ridiculous
Like this
Loud, brash song with lyrics
That make no sense at all
But still we clung to it
Tightly
Making it a small part of our
Identity
Because that's what you do
When you're growing up
And figuring stuff out

    January 4, 2024
    Lenox, Massachusetts

Written while listening to, and inspired by the song "Surfin' Cow" by The Dead Milkmen. Gee whiz, when I was in high school, I *loved* this song. It actually has pretty good music, but the lyrics are weird, yell-y, and make no sense at all – exactly the kind of thing a teenager latches onto. When I was in Scouts, we even called our patrol at summer camp, The Surfin' Cow Patrol. I still have the (surprisingly impressive) flag.

January

Articles Like This Always Come In Pairs

When seeing an article
On the local paper's website
About a new business opening
With a photograph showing
The proud owners posing
Behind the counter
My mind speeds forward
To a date not far in the future
Where there's another article
That's much much smaller
And buried back a few pages
Mentioning how it was closing
Usually with little to no notice
And, if they could be reached
The owners bitterly blamed
This, that, or the other thing
For the demise of their dream
Because articles like this
Always come in pairs
Yes, separated by years,
But the second one
Will inevitably come

>January 4, 2024
>Lenox, Massachusetts

I saw an article* on the local paper's website about a new business opening where a previous business closed a few years ago. These young new owners were very optimistic about being able to make a go of it where the previous owners failed. This is where my mind fast forwards a couple of years to read about the new business closing.

Written while listening to "Senseless Fun" by Dramarama.

*Actually, just a headline. I don't pay to have full access to the site.**

***I know!* I'm so bad.

January

Fishing For A Job

Fishing for a job
Sitting in my boat
Alone
Not getting any bites
But enjoying the view
Not as concerned
About landing a career
Like I once did
When I was obsessive
About doing my best
Trying to impress
All those above me
By working days off
Overtime covering
For the lackluster others
But this time out here
Sitting on the water
Has made me rethink
My priorities and what
It is that I truly want
And it's not spending
All of my free time
Furthering my career
Killing myself for
A company that couldn't care
Any less for their employees
And wouldn't notice
If I dropped dead one day
So, this time away
Has given me perspective
And made me realize
That we should be
Living our lives *for us*
Not living our lives *to work* –
To bring gobs of profit
To some giant corporation,
But to *live* and do

The Comfortable In-Between

What we want –
To enrich our experience,
Not enrich your boss
And the company they live for

        January 7, 2024
        Lenox, Massachusetts

Written while listening to "So Weit" by Urbs, and "New Romantics (Taylor's Version)" by Taylor Swift.

January

As We Clean

Snow
Light and
Fluffy
Barely there
Seemingly
Weightless
Making it
Easy
To sweep
To shovel
To move
Elsewhere
As we clean
The areas
We need to
Go through
So we can
Enjoy the view
But still get
Elsewhere
Easily

January 7, 2024
Lenox, Massachusetts

We got about eight or nine inches of snow.

Written while listening to "No Cars Go" by Arcade Fire.

The Scenery Outside

Finally
The day has come
Where the season
On the calendar
Actually matches
The scenery outside
Instead of a season
Ahead or behind

                January 7, 2024
                Lenox, Massachusetts

Written while listening to "Introduction / Hey Betty" by Dramarama.

I'm listening to my "Liked Songs" playlist (1,588 songs) on Spotify, so I'm getting some songs I normally don't hear when I'm writing. I normally listen only to my "Poetry Mix" (126 hours of music – I'm not sure why one playlist tells me how many songs there on in it, but another playlist just tells me how many hours it is).

January

The Slow Fade To Night

The slow fade to night
Where you spend time
Squinting at things
Until you realize
It'd be much easier
To just turn on the light
Where everything outside
Dims down to a grayish-blue
Even the carpet of snow below
Undisturbed by the romping squirrels
Who have left and gone to bed
Same with the little birds
That have swarmed to my feeder
All gone elsewhere
To snug up and sleep
While the light fades more
And everything is now
Just black and white
With a slightly cold tinge to it
As dots of lights appear
From neighbors who are home
Not aware and not caring
About the draining light
As we push forward into night

January 7, 2024
Lenox, Massachusetts

Written while listening to "Automatic Buffalo" by The Sheila Divine.

The Skull People

You know the type –
It's always a truck
With various versions
Of the American flag
With each and every one
Violating the US Flag Code
Being distorted
Or discolored
In some way
Usually showing it
Ragged or frayed
But it doesn't stop there
The skull people
Always have stickers
Showing excarnation –
Which always confused me
Why would anyone want
The symbol they're choosing
To stand behind
To apply to them
Be a skull, of all things?
Are they trying to say
They have no vision?
Did they select this
Because it has no brain?
A severed head
Without use of a body
With absolutely no ability
To grasp anything
To move anywhere
Or even live
Seems to be a strange thing
To want to identify with
But, if I had to guess,
They would probably think
It shows they're tough
And see themselves as killers

January

And dangerous people
When in reality
In a normal society
They're just laughable
Tough-guy cosplayers
Sadly, bound by the rule of law

        January 10, 2024
        Lenox, Massachusetts

So silly. It's like the people who trick out their cars so they can go super-fast, when in reality we have speed limits and they can't even use their cars (legally) to their full potential. These guys I wrote about are all about guns, freedum, and trying to be a "tough guy," appearing (in their minds) like a badass, when they're just laughable. Oh, what are you going to do…actually shoot someone? No. You would go to jail. But…you can make people think you're someone who has no regard for life and *would* kill someone, if crossed. All these people deserve to be mocked relentlessly.

Written while listening to "Insomniac Olympics" by Blockhead.

Retaliation

Retaliation
Is just a
Continuation
Of past wrongs
Real or imaginary
Perpetuating
The terrible cycle
With no one involved
Willing to pause
Or learn from history

    January 12, 2024
    Lenox, Massachusetts

Written while listening to "Let's Make A Mistake Tonight" by Tennis.

January

Betterment

Why can't we
Take the best ideas
From all of the
Towns, cities,
States, countries,
Study all there is
To offer the rest of us,
And universally
Adopt the ideas
The ones that
Are really proven
The ones that work
To level up
To make everyplace
Just a bit better
It doesn't matter
Where they're from
Or who implemented them
Or how much profit
Can be made from it
Just Good Ideas Only
For the betterment
Of our entire society and
For the good of humanity

    January 12, 2024
    Lenox, Massachusetts

We were watching a walking video on YouTube by "Scenes By Sevy." He lives in Finland and it's fascinating looking at things like how the small towns and cities are laid out, and the real, honest, seemingly "people-first" way of doing things, from extra wide sidewalks, to the street lighting, to the recycling bins, to the neighborhood parking garages, and more. It reminds me of how Rick Steves says that "traveling is a political act" because you come back changed from what you see and experience. It just makes me wish we could remove ourselves from our death-grip on the need to always be profiting off of everything.

Written while listening to "Sleepy Maggie" by Ashley MacIsaac.

January

Traces

The memories we have
The traces we leave
Physically,
Mentally,
Emotionally,
From the touch
On, and beyond
The moments
Framed with lights
And the blur
Of the world
Passing by
The main story
Of our lives
Moving by
Much too quickly
Like grabbing
Handfuls of water
The coldness fading
The wetness drying
But the knowledge
And the memory
Is still burning bright
Brighter, so brightly
Even as the pages
Of the calendar
Flip on by
So, we still
Keep grabbing
Keep trying
To hold tightly
To the moment
To keep it from
Fading, diminishing
And never ever
Let it go completely
Because that's like

The Comfortable In-Between

Giving up
Which is something
We can never do
Not when the traces
Are still here
And are still so real

                  January 12, 2024
                  Lenox, Massachusetts

The song "Fool's Gold" by Dagny came on my playlist and I just wrote to the feeling of it.

January

The Essential Elemental Me

Time to get back
To basics
Time to find out
What is the
Essential
Elemental me
The most distilled
The most elevated
Fundamental
Core version
Of myself
Because
When I get there
To that place
Of alignment
With my
Wispy floaty
Soul self
Is when
Everything aligns,
Manifestation ensues
Magic happens
And nothing but
Pure joy
Radiates
From that place

Buuut…

Chances are still
Pretty good
That I'll have to
Endure the banalities
Of daily life
Like lines, bad drivers,
And frustrations
But hopefully

The Comfortable In-Between

I'll be a little bit happier
And, in the end,
Isn't that
What we want?

        January 12, 2024
        Lenox, Massachusetts

Written while listening to "The Heinrich Maneuver" by Interpol on repeat.

January

Roof Down

Sportscar turning
Rounding the corner
Roof down but
Windows up
Despite it being
Mid-January
Despite it being
Just about freezing
Making me wonder
Were they doing it
Due to
Alcoholic intoxication?
Mechanical malfunction?
Plain old chionophile?
Or all of the above?
I don't know
But on this day,
In these conditions,
It just seems wrong

        January 19, 2024
        Lenox, Massachusetts

True story.

Written while listening to "All The Sad Young Men" by Spector.

The Houses Are Starting To Come Down

The houses
Are starting
To come down
Torn apart
In large chunks
With each swipe
From the steel
Power paw
From the yellow Cat
Driving past
Seeing through
The glassless windows
Seeing light
Never seen to that extent
In those rooms ever before
As the roof was already gone
As the back wall was down
Heaped on the ground
As the Cat swiped again
Knocking loose more floor.
As I ran my errands
I thought about that house
Currently dying on my street
And I got to thinking
About the people who built it
Back in 1900
About the people who bought it
And how happy they must have been
To move into this brand-new house
And how modern it must have been
And the generations of families
That grew up, got old, passed on
This home of theirs
Again and again
Never thinking of
Never expecting
The possibility

January

That this day
Could, or would
Ever come
To them,
This house
Which sheltered them
Which protected them
Which served them all
Faithfully for so long
Would ever be deemed
Unusable, unworkable,
Useless, and be torn down
Unceremoniously
To make way
For a car dealership
On a cold January day
In the impossibly
Incomprehensible year
Of 2024
But here we are.
My errands done,
I drive past the house again
And all that's left is one corner
Two stories
One window
Standing proud
Standing tall
As if it knew
It had done a good job
Taking one last look
At the view it knew
For the last 124 years
As the backhoe gave it
One last powerful hit
Knocking the remainder
Over, tumbling down
Joining the rest of the rubble
That will be scooped up
And eventually carted away

The Comfortable In-Between

To be completely forgotten
Once the shiny new dealership
Is built and open

                January 19, 2024
                Lenox, Massachusetts

A BMW dealership from Pittsfield wanted to move to Lenox, but to do it, they had to buy and tear down five or six houses and a couple of businesses. The fancy kitchen store building (A Different Drummer Kitchen) was torn down the other day. Now, they're working on the houses. It just got me thinking about what was once there, and how we think of things like our home as something that will always be there but, eventually, they'll all meet the same fate. When I was a kid, our family would be in the car driving to this or that, and my father would point at a building and say that when he was a kid in the 1940s, his family lived there above a butcher shop, or they lived there in another building. I don't know, it just makes you stop and wonder about the people who lived in, were excited about, enjoyed a place, and how eventually, someone will buy that place to tear it down.

Written while listening to "The Funeral" by Band of Horses on repeat.

January

A Deluge In The Desert

When it rains
It pours
A deluge in the desert
After a year of nothing
Where the weather thinks
Like a bad plant parent
Who forgot to water
The plant in the corner
For far far too long
And then, overcompensates
By practically submerging it
In more than it can handle
Western-state-like dryness
Now afflicted with
Constant tsunamis
With water coming from
Every possible direction
Making it necessary
To say no again and again
Every day, all day long

    January 19, 2024
    Lenox, Massachusetts

For over a year now, I've been applying for jobs. I've been choosy; carefully applying for only positions I've been 100% qualified for, and being thoughtful with writing a new cover letter for each. 60+ jobs later, I've gotten nothing. Well, that's not entirely true – I've been offered a few jobs, but have turned them down for various reasons. Now, for some reason, I've been getting interview requests every day. I've had three awesome interviews this week with another two planned for next week. Chances are great, I'll get hired in the next week or so, but I wanted to write about how it feels.

The Comfortable In-Between

Written while listening to "While You Wait For The Others" by Grizzly Bear.

January

The Job Of The Dark

The job of the light
Is to show you what
It is you need to see
The job of the dark
Is to be guiding you
To know the difference
Experience the contrast
To have understanding
Of the entire picture

        January 21, 2024
        Lenox, Massachusetts

Written while listening to "Elsewhere" by Sarah McLachlan.

The Most Powerful Thing

Sometimes a cat's paw
Reaching out and touching
Your hand or your arm
Is the most powerful thing
Making you change your mind
And making you change your plans
As you are now tasked
With one thing:
Giving pets

                        January 21, 2024
                        Lenox, Massachusetts

January

Watching The Day Pass

Watching the day pass
The shadows ringing around
The holes in the snow
Made by romping squirrels
Morning, noon, afternoon
The source of light
Gliding on by
From the south side
Shadowing long and low
Until it all stretches out
When the sun is extinguished
And everything becomes a shadow

            January 21, 2024
            Lenox, Massachusetts

Consider A New Path

The succinct lines
That eloquently act
As the apt summation
Of the emotional equivalency
Of nutritional perfection
Where, once ingested,
By the open, ready,
And deeply desiring ears,
Each word individually
Each word building
Is completely fulfilling
Is striking a chord
Deeply reverberating
Severely shaking
Always, like the bass
Causing the kind of feeling
That gets you
Right in the heart
Right in the center
Of your entire being
Shaking your core
Earthquaking you
To awareness
Of new possibilities
Never considered
Making you want to
Consider a new path

January 21, 2024
Lenox, Massachusetts

January

The Flooding

The flooding
Coming from
The thawing
And stepping
Away from
The chilling
Just for a day
Is enough to
Make this
A new thing
Embracing
The warmth
So looking
Forward to
This warmth
Melting things
Making things
So different
So dramatically
Changed
For the better
Freshining
The landscape
Invigorating
The senses
Deadened
By the snow
Which covered
And froze
All that we see
But now
With the heat
Movement
Has returned
Movement
Has inspired
Change, for

The Comfortable In-Between

As the land
Changes, so
In fact, do we
So we embrace
The newness
The impending
Season which is
Blossoming
All around
And with it
Comes our
Celebrating
Of the flooding
Because it's what
Gives us all life

        January 21, 2024
        Lenox, Massachusetts

For the past week it's been really cold and this coming week it'll warm up to about 50 (10 Celsius), so we should see most, if not all, of the snow we have melt. I know flooding from snow melt can cause problems, but at least we have water here and are not suffering from a terrible drought like the western half of the country. Also, I saw a tree the other day covered in buds, like it was springtime.

Written while listening to "Southpaw" by Morrissey.

January

Interruptions

The interruptions
Constantly prying
Me apart
From the process
Sidetracking
Derailing
Each and every time
Like an avalanche
Blocking the highway
Making me abandon
The route I was going
Having to find
A new way there
And, eventually,
I finally get moving
Happily speeding along
Until it happens again
Stopping me in my tracks
Head hanging low
Temporarily defeated
I, again, have to get over it
Figure out a new way to go
And find the motivation
To re-start the whole thing
Knowing full well
That it's probably going to
Just happen again
At any moment

January 21, 2024
Lenox, Massachusetts

The Comfortable In-Between

January

The Comfortable In-Between

FEBRUARY

February

A Level Head Should Have Been In Charge

You can't build on the flames
Of the thing you burned down
Rebuilding can only really begin
Once the ashes have finally cooled
And that is when
The realization begins
That maybe, just maybe
A level head should have been in charge
And not the mindless, heartless hand
In charge of holding the torch

        February 3, 2024
        Lenox, Massachusetts

Written while listening to "The Moon Is In The Wrong Place" by Shannon & The Clams.

The City

The city
So busy
Seemingly full
Packed bursting
People standing
Walking, hanging out
Everywhere you look
Those visiting
From the places
That are mostly green
With no concrete in sight
Lock their car doors
While stopped at a red light
Not knowing, not understanding
What they're seeing
Because, for them,
It's just too much
In the way of humanity
Crowding their line of sight
Because this "too much"
Is completely foreign
To their unacquainted senses
But
Instead of relaxing,
Taking all of it in,
Seeking more of this,
And allowing this experience
To be expanding their worldview
They continue to remain small
Mentally, emotionally, culturally
And off they go
Back to the safety
And lack of diversity
Of their known territory

> February 3, 2024
> Lenox, Massachusetts

February

For my mom's birthday (tomorrow), we took her to Red Rose Pizza in downtown Springfield (which was great!). While there, I took in the downtown of the largest city in western Massachusetts and thought how this kind of urban setting would make those who are used to rural environments scared and want to get home as soon as possible, even though it was a totally normal and not scary place. I remember last year taking the train from upstate New York into Manhattan and seeing another passenger who had obviously never been to the city stare wide-eyed at the graffiti and the people we passed by.

Written while listening to "My Favorite Mutiny" by The Coup.

The Comfortable In-Between

We Should Watch Bake Off Instead

Excited for a newly discovered show
That's been on for decades
And how we've got twenty-four seasons
Of this English murder mystery show
To watch, and catch up on
But, it also makes me a little worried
As we excitedly talk aloud
About how we can't wait
For another "Murder"
And how much we love
Murder murder murder
Wondering what the devices
We have that listen
To our every word
So they can better
Suggest advertisements
And better predict
What we will want to buy
What exactly these devices
Like our TV and our phones
Will do with this new information
Will they tip off the police
About our new-found evening excitement?
Are they inviting other law enforcement
To also listen in on what we say?
Just as a precaution; just in case?
I honestly have no idea
So maybe, just maybe
We should watch Bake Off instead

    February 3, 2024
    Lenox, Massachusetts

Written while listening to "Gay Sons of Lesbian Mothers" by Kaki King.

February

The Kind Of Opportunity

Changing places
Changing times
Choosing something
Challenging and different
Where the peaks
Are snow-covered
And razor-sharp
And the valleys
Are thick, dense,
And chock-full of life
As an alternative
To the same-old
Bland, boring
Flavorless ordinary
Experienced daily
In the current life
A serious shake-up of things
To get down to new ground
Widening the understanding
Enhancing the attaining
Leveling up to heights
Previously unknown
And unconsidered
As an actual possibility
The kind of opportunity
That changes everything

                February 3, 2024
                Lenox, Massachusetts

Written while listening to "Rolling Waves" by The Naked And Famous.

Anvil Of Consequences

Flyer in the mail
Too big in size
Too many colors
Too similar in look
To the game Monopoly
Showing a cartoon figure
Of a man with a big moustache
Of train engines, of top hats,
Of antique race cars
Everything even in the font
They use in the famous game
But all of it just different enough
To make sure they don't get sued
By the famous game's owner
This should have been
My first red flag
That this was a scam
Most of the flyer
Was brashly proclaiming
About their eight-day sale
But the part that caught
My deep interest was the game
A section where you peeled away
Three tabs and if what was under
Matched the Monopoly-like symbols
Over on the right, then you WON
And when I did it, I won $500
Which, of course, seemed
Entirely too good to be true
So, I read all of the fine print
And nothing there indicated
That there was any tomfoolery
Or anything sketchy or scammy
I just had to go to a website
Enter my contact information
Plus a code from the mailer
And schedule an appointment

February

At the dealership directly
To go and pick up my prize
Which is what I did, right away
And half an hour later, there I was
At the Nissan dealership
And when I walked in
I felt like I was in for
Something low-rent
Something kind of scammy
As twenty to thirty men
(Every one of them, a man)
Stood to the sides
Of the showroom floor
Laughing and guffawing
Entirely too loudly
While others were setting up
Plastic folding tables
And setting out
Plastic folding chairs
While someone else dropped
Piles of half sheets of paper
Re-photocopied over and over
Too often, for too many years
The words were grainy
And slightly blurry
And more than a little askewy
But that no longer mattered
Because this was a form
Meant to collect information
From the incoming innocents
And, by the looks of it,
They were clearly expecting
A really big turnout today
I barely had time to take it all in
When a friendly man
In a puffy vest shook my hand
Introduced himself
And asked me to sit
He started out by copying down

The Comfortable In-Between

My address information
From the flyer I had brought in
That they had sent me
Showing I had won
But that's not what he cared about
Or what he looked at –
Just my address information
They can use to bulk up
Their mailing lists
And those of third parties
They can sell my information to
And then he sat down
And was telling me about
How great their cars are
And asked me all about mine
The year, make, and model
The mileage, where I bought it
How much I paid per month
How much I still owe on it
And then pulled a number
Right out of his ass
Giving an amount
If I wanted to trade it in
That was many thousands more
Than I paid for the car
Four years ago
An amount, I'm sure,
They would never give
Had I taken him up on it
Just trying to get me
To open up on the idea
To sell my fine car
And get into one of theirs
(The whole point of all this)
Eventually, he took my flyer
And looked up a code
That was by my address
And nowhere near the game
Or the area showing my prize

February

He pointed at a foam-core poster
Listing all the fabulous cash prizes
Saying I was a WINNER
And I would be getting five dollars
I pointed at the flyer
At the area that showed
I was indeed a WINNER
And I had won five hundred dollars
He said that the amounts listed
Don't correspond to the symbols
And only the code matters
And I had won five dollars
Taking my winning flyer
He handed me a $5 bill
Standing from the table
And biding me a good day
In a polite, yet firm way to say
It's time for you to leave
I stated that this was
A clear case of bait and switch
And left, knowing I would get
Absolutely nowhere dealing
With this guy, or any of the others
Still laughing and talking loudly
Around the edges of the floor
I left
Pissed beyond belief
That I had been scammed
So blatantly
By people
So unashamedly
Doing this again and again
All day long to everyone
Who genuinely thought
Their luck had turned
And they had won
Hundreds, if not
Thousands of dollars
And made the trip

To this dealership
To claim their winnings
Only to be told
Nope, not for you.

When I got home
I thought I would
Actually do something
To try and fix things
Because this isn't right
For them to be
Scamming people
Using Nissan's name
So I looked it up
On Nissan's website
And found a big list
Of their North American executives
And, from there, found the ones
Whose jobs would pertain specifically
To what I had just gone through
And wrote to three vice presidents
With photos of the flyer
And deeply described
What had transcribed
And asked for my personal information
That the dealership required from me
To be deleted and not sold
To any third party
And I hope that something
Akin to an anvil of consequences
Or other densely heavy weight
Will be dropped from their corporate offices
And land on those at the dealership
Who came up with this scamming plan

Even now, as I write this
They are texting me
From an area code
Somewhere in Ohio

February

Asking me to come in
To claim my prize
Because I'm a WINNER

        February 11, 2024
        Lenox, Massachusetts

I believe in the power of the anvil of consequences.

Note: no one replied to my emails. They did, however, almost lose their license and were forced to sell for doing lots of other scammy things.

A Lot Early

Spring has arrived
A little early
Actually,
A *lot* early
Six weeks or so
And I'm sitting
On my porch
Enjoying the warmth
Wearing short sleeves
Seeing bugs
Newly awakened
Flying lazily past
Smelling the freshness
The complex earthiness
Of the ground
Working on thawing
Preparing the land
For the season to come
Enjoying the moment
Until I look at my weather app
And see that winter
Returns with a fierceness
The day after tomorrow
Pausing the warmth
And hiding all of this
Under a pile of snow

               February 11, 2024
               Lenox, Massachusetts

Written while listening to "Fangela" by Here We Go Magic.

February

Lentil Soup

It's so strange
To be thinking
That someday
There will be
Strangers touching
Possibly judging
The can and the brand
Of lentil soup
In your cupboard
That you bought one day
Fully intending to eat
At some point soon
But then, you died
And here's that can
In a stranger's hand
A few months later
During the inspection
Of the home you owned
And how you never thought
That the can of soup
Could somehow outlive you

    February 14, 2024
    Lenox, Massachusetts

Written while listening to "Sanskrit Prayers" by Chaula Hopefisher. The person who previously owned the house we are buying was a new age musician. She passed away a few months ago and it seems so strange to see things as simple as a can of soup and to think that she planned on eating this can of soup, but died before she could. It just makes you stop and think.

The song mentioned above was made by the house's previous owner. She had an amazing voice, and I will say the house has a really positive energy to it.

The Idea Is Forming

The idea
Is forming
The direction
Is solidifying
Movement
Is impending
Despite the
Rapid passing
Of seconds
Of minutes
Of years
Blurring by

                    February 14, 2024
                    Lenox, Massachusetts

February

Dear Universe

Dear Universe
From this point on
I'm no longer letting
Stupid inane shit
Stand in my way
Prevent me from doing
The things I want
From going in
The directions I desire
Spending time worrying
About what others
Might or might not say
Or think is something
That should never stop
The spark of creativity
From lighting and flickering
Providing warmth and light
To those who need it
From inspiring others
From creating their own
Sparks forming a burning
Banding together, spreading
The messages, extinguishing
The fear that held us down
Uplifting all who see
The bonfires created by those
Who refused to let others
Smother the spark
Before it had a chance
To ignite and alight
Every one of us

February 14, 2024
Lenox, Massachusetts

Written while listening to "Speak In Rounds" by Grizzly Bear.

What's In The Dock

Whenever I see a video showing
A creative person's computer
I always like to look to see
What's in the dock
(Because it's always a Mac)
Is it just the programs
That came standard
With the computer?
Is it sparsely populated
Meaning they don't do a lot?
Or, is it so heavily crowded
That the icons are nearly invisible?
I also get excited when I see
The same programs as me
Meaning we're on similar paths
And that, for some reason,
Gives me a lot of comfort

February 14, 2024
Lenox, Massachusetts

Written while listening to "More Important Than Michael Jordan" by Pretty Lights.

February

It Must Be Now

Stopping
Is not an option
Is not something
I can do
Even though
I may want to
Just pause
And rest
But the drive
The fire
Burns brightly within
And without regard
To things like
Clocks or time
It simply is something
That must be done
If not now
Then perhaps never
So, it must be now

        February 14, 2024
        Lenox, Massachusetts

After the last one, I was about to stop, because I have a weird thing where I will only write an even number of poems in a sitting, but the idea of this shoved its way through my mind and compelled me to keep writing.

I started writing this while still listening to "More Important Than Michael Jordan" by Pretty Lights, which I was listening to while writing the previous poem (it's a long song), and finished writing it with "A Sorta Fairytale" by Tori Amos.

Upturned

Upturned
Due to the hope
Still lingering
And motivating
The movement
Despite the worst
Parts of society
Trying their best
To push down
On everything
They don't like
That's not like them
Trying to create fear
In nearly everything
But ignoring
Their actions
Their intentions
Lessens their impact
Depletes their power
Makes them nothing
And allows you
To grow upward
And sprout past
Their regressive nature
And reach your potential

February 14, 2024
Lenox, Massachusetts

Written while listening to "French Press" by Rolling Blackouts Coastal Fever.

A Renewed Flailing

"I am hereby taking a break"
Said the person
On a social app
"There's no way I can do this anymore"
Which is a funny thing to say
Since the very beginning
From day one
They were the person
Who has always been
Chock full of oversharing
And creatively embellishing
Situations, events, and scenarios
Like pressing their own juice
Trying to squeeze the most
Likes, comments, and sympathy
In an over-the-top "woe is me" way
Thickly layered with melodrama
And liberally spiced with agony
Blowing things out of proportion
Until they become bigger than life
And are quickly forgotten
When the next issue pops up
Causing and calling for
A renewed flailing in anguish
As a means for harvesting
Comments expressing empathy

    February 20, 2024
    Lenox, Massachusetts

Written while listening to "Once We Were" by Scraps Of Tape.

Always The Exception

In their minds they are
Always the exception
Living with a mindset
Where the rules just don't
Apply to them
Or anyone
Who they like
Or resemble
Because, to them,
Rules are only there
For Other People
Who are viewed as
Lesser Than
For Other People
Who don't have
The look
The color
The pedigree
The background
The finances
The beliefs
The predilection
To be the same peg as them
Fitting in the same hole
While slaloming past
The complex array of gates,
Rules, and procedures
They have set up
To block
To pause
To stop
Other People
From getting at least this far
But ideally from preventing
Them from getting all the way
To the places they have deemed
As exclusive, where they feel

February

They deserve to be
Away from Other People

> February 20, 2024
> Lenox, Massachusetts

Written while listening to "You Push I'll Go" by Baby Dayliner.

The Phrase Buffet

Holding the thought
Or trying to at least
Because things like this
Can be elusive, slippery
A slimy wriggling fish
Not wanting to be caught
Stronger than anticipated
Thrashing like mad
Like its life depended
On getting away
Just like this thought
Wanting to be by itself
An independent thing
Not beholden to anyone
And here I come along
Snatching it from the water
Depriving it from breathing
Wanting to make it into
Something completely new
Not asked for, not wanted
But here I am just the same
Until it zigs when I assumed
Incorrectly it would be zagging
And it slips from my hands
And completely out of my mind
A notion, an idea, forgotten
But, no worries for me
I'll just wait until another
Swims close enough
However, the thought I lost,
Knows how close it came
To becoming a brief fillet
Just an amuse bouche
In the phrase buffet
That is this book

February 22, 2024

February

Lenox, Massachusetts

Written while listening to "Black Metallic" by Catherine Wheel.

Sanding Down Our Edges

There's an appeal
To the gritty side
Which causes a pause
A hold on our normal
Way of doing things
Maybe it's the allure
Of a chaotic way of life
That we firmly eschew
In our continuous striving
For normalcy
That can be boring,
A life missing
The excitement
Of saying "fuck it"
And abandoning
Responsibilities
Done on a small scale
With using sick days
When going to the beach
But never to the extent
That we, in our core selves,
Truly, deeply crave
A need to feel
Excitement
Passion
Something new
Godammit
Anything
But the same
Day in and day out
That dulls us
Sanding down
Our edges
Over the decades
Until we are
Completely featureless
Which brings us back

February

To the appeal
Stirring the pot
Churning up
The past self
The wants
That once were
So important
The needs
That seemed
Mountainous
Guiding the path
That the life
Would seem to take
But no one anticipates
The societal smooth-down
Continuously grinding
With fine grit
Bit-by-bit
Until what made us
Who we are
Has been completely
And utterly removed

    February 22, 2024
    Lenox, Massachusetts

Written while listening to "Last Night I Dreamt That Somebody Loved Me" by The Smiths.

Spray Painted Snow

Spray painted snow
Outside this morning
Looks like the kind of thing
Used on low-budget movie sets
In the 1980s
To make it look like winter
But, at the same time
They clearly ran out
Around the edges
Which are clearly green
Just enough to cover
The bulk of the ground in a
Somewhat-thick enough white
But is patchy in other parts
Giving it an inauthentic feel
Kind of like nature
Barely tried this time

     February 23, 2024
     Lenox, Massachusetts

Written while listening to "Summer Sun" by Matt Berry.

February

A Mini-Vacation

Closing my eyes
I block out
I release
Everything
Around me
Everything
Holding me
Down
Gravity included
As I shudder
Discard this
Weight, this
Planet,
And ascend
Upward
Past all of this
Upward
Beyond
Where I am
Lighter
Than light
Faster
Than thought
Where I am
Energetic intelligence
Where I seek out
This place
This space
To escape
This life
For a few minutes
To recharge
To rejuvenate
To feel the home
Where I go
Between lives
A tiny excursion

The Comfortable In-Between

A mini-vacation
To revitalize
And then back down
Through the layers
Increasing in density
Until I am, once again
Earth-bound me

        February 23, 2024
        Lenox, Massachusetts

When I meditate.

This is probably a little silly, but after each time I meditate I "grade" my meditation. If I get really distracted and can't stop thinking about stupid stuff and get off-track, I'll give it an F or a D. I think my average is usually about a B. Some are good, some are so-so. Lately, I've been meditating more and they've been A-level powerhouse meditations. Why? I have no idea, but I'll gladly take it.

Written while listening to "Anything You Synthesize" by The American Dollar.

February

Outrunning A Minivan

The new sports car
In the next lane
With the guttural growl
That I expected
To be an asshole
Did not disappoint
Not one bit
As it revved
And sped
Outrunning a minivan
Just to show it can
And then weaved
In and out
Threading through
The sporadic traffic
On their way
To someplace
More important
Much faster
Than we,
And the posted
Speed limit,
Want to go

    February 26, 2024
    Lenox, Massachusetts

Written while listening to "Ohm" by Yo La Tengo.

The Exciting Unknown

The setting sun
Over the western edge
Of the continent
Over the ocean
With the sky
Acting as
The canvas above
Reflecting the light
Displaying the colors
Brightly, a few minutes ago
Dulling, diluting down now
To the faded variants
That signal the night
Approaching
That beckon
Mysterious potential
The exciting unknown
That this evening
Could lead to anything
Resulting in
Lasting memories

    February 26, 2024
    Lenox, Massachusetts

Written while listening to "Coastin'" by Sol Rising.

The vibe of this song made me think of the well-past sunset sky over a California beach town and how it feels to be faced with the amazing, completely unknown potential of an evening.

February

Did The Unthinkable

Stepped out
Of my comfort zone
And did the unthinkable
By interjecting myself
Into someone else's
Private conversation
Offering a helpful answer
To the question
They were unable to solve
Which guided them
To the solution
They needed

        February 26, 2024
        Lenox, Massachusetts

When I'm out and about, I really stay to myself and minimize interaction with others. Why? I don't know. It's probably the Frostian New Englandy mindset of "Good fences make good neighbors." Today, I was at Target and an older woman, and her much older mother were looking at their shopping list which had the CLR brand cleaner on it, but neither of them knew what it was or where to find it. I was nearby spending far too much time mentally weighing the pros and cons of the various features of cat litter when I interrupted and told them what CLR was, and where to find it. It was me stepping out of my comfort zone and doing something I normally don't do.

Written while listening to "Shotgun" by Soccer Mommy.

The Certainty

The certainty associated with
The importance of knowing
Is quite the combination
Marching hand-in-hand
In a fully confident way
That assuredly indicates
"Hey. I know what I'm doing.
 I've got this."

                February 26, 2024
                Lenox, Massachusetts

Written while listening to "I Wanna Be Your Dog" by John McCrea (*Cruella* Soundtrack).

February

A Mind Changed

A mind changed
An idea abandoned
A poem deleted
Never to be seen
Just as if it had
Never existed

        February 28, 2024
        Lenox, Massachusetts

I had an idea for a poem that I wrote a good amount of notes for the other day, but tonight when I was reviewing them, I thought better of it and deleted it.

Written while listening to "The Streets" by Double Vision.

The Comfortable In-Between

A Hand Reaching Long

The first notes
Of this song
Strikes hard
Like a hand
Reaching long
Through time
Across thirty years
From the young me
With an optimist's eye
To the wrinkled now
With the wisdom to know
Better than before
But still, it reaches
And knocks on my heart
With each rapping
Causes the same skipping
Striking me where it counts
Affecting me deeply
Causing pause
Trying to inspire
Deep reflection
But I am too smart for that now
And I choose to skip
The feelings,
This song,
And with the abrupt change
From that song to another
I am freed
And allowed
To go about my day
Unscathed by
The musical ghosts
That lurk in the past

    February 28, 2024
    Lenox, Massachusetts

February

Written while listening to "Something's Always Wrong" by Toad The Wet Sprocket.

There are a few songs I've always kept together due to their powerful impact on me. Just after college, I made a mixed CD of them called "Southpaw" after the Morrissey song. This Toad The Wet Sprocket song has always caused me to "have the feels" as the kids would say, for no reason other than I always would get swept up in the music and the lyrics on this one. I have always been more into the music and the feeling the music inspires. Honestly don't know the words to most of my favorite songs, but this one I do, and I can't help but to sing it when it plays.

Sidenote: I kept hitting CMD-S to save this poem every couple of words as I was writing it. Today was nearly 60 degrees (15.5 C) and the temperature is dropping 45 degrees in three hours, and with it, high winds with gusts up to 60 mph (96.5 kph). The power has flickered a few times, so I was afraid of losing what I've written tonight – hence the frequent saving.

The Comfortable In-Between

MARCH

Paper Date

For those
Born on
February
Twenty-ninth
In person
They are
Aged
By the date
Impossibly
Young
As much
As they laugh
About being
Twelve
On paper
With each
Successive day
They wish
Much harder
For the
Paper date
To be true

>March 1, 2024
>Lenox, Massachusetts

Yesterday was Leap Year Day, so it was time for all of the news articles interviewing old people whose official age is that of a teen.

Written while listening to "Sometimes Wanna Die" by Joydrop.

March

Richly Lived Elsewhere

The allure
Of a life
Richly lived
Elsewhere
Is so powerful
Until you reach it
And the "there"
Is now your "here"
And, instead of
Running from
All your problems
You've conveniently
Brought them with you
In your oversized baggage
So now, the new place
Is exactly like the old place
But with different scenery

        March 1, 2024
        Lenox, Massachusetts

Written while listening to "Gravel" by Ani DiFranco.

Naming Rights For Disasters

Considering the direction
That our society is heading
I would not be the least surprised
If the powers that be start selling
The naming rights for disasters
With disasters, big and small,
Having ridiculous names like
Tsunami Brawny™
Volcano Reynolds Wrap™
Mudslide Kahlua™
Polar vortex Fla-Vor-Ice™
Wildfire Char-Broil™
And Earthquake Hitachi Magic Wand™
The only unbelievable part of this
Is that they're not already doing this

                March 5, 2024
                Lenox, Massachusetts

Written while listening to "Suburban War" by Arcade Fire.

March

The Collection Of Things

The collection of things
We choose to surround
Ourselves with
Serves both
As a definition
Of who we are
And a deep study
Of what kind of person
We are underneath
That quickly affixed label

        March 5, 2024
        Lenox, Massachusetts

After writing this, I instinctively looked around the office (at the piles of papers and other crap) and thought about me in regards to this one.

Written while listening to "Blue Jeans – Penguin Prison Remix" by Lana Del Rey.

The Words Are The Paints

The page is the canvas
The words are the paints
Black in color on paper
Until they hit the mind
And form the images
Hopefully indelibly
Imprinting the scenes
On the understanding,
And still reading, brain
Filling the world with
Unlimited potential

                    March 5, 2024
                    Lenox, Massachusetts

Written while listening to "Sweet Baby" by Think Of England.

March

Ever Since The Line

Officially
And publicly:
You get used to it
And life continues.
Personally
And mentally:
You don't
And it doesn't
As everything
Is now defined
As "before"
And "after"
Ever since the line
Cut normal life
Cleanly and clearly
In half
Never to be rejoined

        March 5, 2024
        Lenox, Massachusetts

Covid and everything that has been inflicted since. Insert any terrible, life-altering event here. Last week I went to an adult Lego meetup group and it was interesting that, four years on, I kept hearing the phrase "Before Covid" at least a dozen times that evening. It was truly a line in all of our lives.

Written while listening to "Here With Me" by Dido.

Building Fences

Boundaries
Expected
Placed
By others
Surrounding
Singling
Targeting
Just you
They expect
Just you
To live by
Their morals
The same ones
They don't follow
But still they
Go about their days
Building fences
Trying to contain
Everyone
And anyone
They judge
Needing of restriction

    March 7, 2024
    Lenox, Massachusetts

Written while listening to "Um, Circles And Squares" by Dosh.

March

Scenes Seen

All of the places
I've been
All of the things
I've seen
Play out like
A strange movie
When I think about
A certain scene
And realize
It was well over
Twenty years ago
Which seems like
A lifetime in the past
Yet it was something
A moment in time
That I lived through
Such a varied collection
Snippets taken in
Nearly every state
Scenes seen from
All over the world
Sunsets and rises
In exotic locations
Interesting experiences
Happened randomly
Completely by chance
All of it exists here
In my mind
For only me
To see
And re-live
Whenever I want
Which, I guess
Is the true joy
Of experience
And a richly-lived life

The Comfortable In-Between

March 7, 2024
Lenox, Massachusetts

I am not bragging. I just got to thinking about how fortunate I've been to have been and seen so much.

Written while listening to "Bright Side" by John Easdale.

March

Unable To Comprehend Depth

It is more than a little ironic
That those who believe in
And froth at the mouth
At the concept of a "deep state"
Are among the shallowest
And most exceedingly basic
Members of society
Unable to comprehend depth
Even if they were drowning in it
Which they most certainly are
As they happily chomp at the bit
On the hook, line, and sinker
And are completely taken for a ride

    March 7, 2024
    Lenox, Massachusetts

Gloriously Enchanting

Brightly scented candles
Dimmed lights
Great music
Good moods
Laughs all around
Nice drinks
Effervescent smiles
Easy breezy conversation
That, if left going,
Would continue
Until the daylight
One of those nights
Straight from a movie
From back in the sixties
Gloriously enchanting
In every possible way
The perfect conditions for
Incubating a connection
That will last longer
Than time itself

    March 7, 2024
    Lenox, Massachusetts

Written while listening to "Feriado" by Cornelio.

All I had to hear was the first few seconds of this song and I got the whole feeling for this poem. Seriously, go to my Spotify playlist for this poetry collection and listen to this song while reading it.

March

Old Notes

Old notes
Steering me wrong
Tricking me
Making me start
To write something
Again, but different
This time
Despite the idea
Being alarmingly familiar
I still began gearing up
Mentally processing
The notion
Weighing the options
Beginning to plan
All of the routes
This idea could take
As I circumnavigated
The concept's shape
Until something inside
Said, "Wait. Hold up."
And I looked at what I wrote
A few days ago
And there it was
The fully formed idea
Nicely and neatly done
Properly packaged
As its own poem
Not needing a sequel
Or even a remake

        March 14, 2024
        Lenox, Massachusetts

In my Notes app on my phone, I saw the line "naming rights for disasters" and started to run with it. Thankfully, before I got far, I looked on my list of poems I've written this month and saw I had already done it.

Written while listening to "Confusing Possibilities" by The Six Parts Seven.

March

Powerfully Struck

Not having to clean up
After the emotional wreck
That was left when the car
Drunkenly slurred its way
Chaotically across the lines
Hitting cars and trees
Damagingly wandering
All about town
Plowing into everything
Imprinting onto everyone
Who came into contact
With the disastrous driver
But thankfully, not me
As I was ejected long ago
Having smartly not worn
A seat belt – flying by
The seat of my pants
Without any regard
To the direction
We were heading in
Back then, at the time,
Just happy to be there
Along for the ride
Which got too fast
For my enjoyment
And my constant need
To remain staying safe
When stop signs were run
And then, after the fact,
Brakes were slammed
To avert an accident
And out the window I went
Landing safely in the street
Watching the car carom
On down the road
Like a pool ball
Powerfully struck

The Comfortable In-Between

Bouncing and not stopping
The rider gone
The driver
Completely oblivious
They were alone
But that's okay
For me
As I found a ride
And was able to get
To new places
To better places
Previously undreamt
All without
Unhinged drama and
Disastrous consequences

        March 14, 2024
        Lenox, Massachusetts

Written while listening to "Transatlanticism" by Death Cab For Cutie.

I love really long songs like this (7:55) that you can really get into while they build in intensity. I could listen to this song on a loop for hours.

March

Echoes In The Darkness

The echoes in the darkness
The fading reverberation
The thoughts repeating
The regrets resurfacing
As the miles blend and blur
With the only friend
The only true constant
Out here
In the middle of
Nowhere
Being the white shoulder line
Keeping everything going
Steadily and safely
While driving away
From the past
While driving to
Anywhere…
Fast

        March 14, 2024
        Lenox, Massachusetts

The song, "Caroline" by Concrete Blonde came on and it is just so powerful. Whenever I hear it, I feel like I'm in a car, zooming somewhere, on an empty highway in vastness of the Southwest with mile after mile slipping past while someone with a whole lot on their mind pushes the car onward, endlessly. This is what it's like when the right song comes on at the right time – the poem just writes itself.

Ha! I spelled "reverberation" correctly the first time.

The Thermometer Is The One Who Calls It

The first spring day
Was today
Even though on paper
It isn't for another week
But, the thermometer
Is the one who calls it,
Along with the smell
In the air
The fresh one
The yawning one
Waking up
Shaking off
The dullened senses
Along with the
Increased activity
Of neighbors
Whom I haven't seen
Since the fall
Out in their yards
Picking up sticks
Starting burn piles
Sending the sweet
Smokey aroma
Into the air
Signaling the start
Of spring
Of something new

    March 14, 2024
    Lenox, Massachusetts

True story.

Written while listening to "Where Do We Go" by Blue Sky Black Death.

March

By My Side

Love is
A scaredy
Skittish cat
Being brave
Enough to
Hang out
By my side
Because he
Wants to be
Here with me

        March 15, 2024
        Lenox, Massachusetts

Welton the cat (AKA Sir Welton Fluffytail) is curled up on a big square poof thing beside me while I'm at the computer. His previous owners lied about and vastly overstated his personality to the shelter we got him from (probably to make sure he got adopted right away, which is what happened). He is a wonderful, loving cat, and it's taken nine months so far for him to slooooooowly open up to us, with tiny gains every day. It's nice to have such a scaredy cat finally feel so completely comfortable with us.

Written while listening to "Julian" by Say Lou Lou.

The Comfortable In-Between

Spend More Time

There is so much wrong
So much that's messed up
With this world
We're all trapped on
Which makes me wonder
Why I don't choose
To spend more time
Meditating, just to get away
And go back home
To the life between lives
Even for just twenty minutes
To feel weight of the world
Just melt away
And become weightless
While soaking in the energy
Recharging, refilling, refreshing me
The needed bit of balance
Tipping me back to normalcy
Allowing me to be more even
Giving that spark
Brightening my day

    March 15, 2024
    Lenox, Massachusetts

Written while listening to "Anti-Hero" by Taylor Swift.

March

The Generically Named

The generically named
Have a tendency
To vanish completely
Into the internet
Never to be found again

        March 19, 2024
        Lenox, Massachusetts

Written while listening to "Free" by edapollo.

I feel like I have to comment here about the songs I listen to. I don't choose a song based on what I'm going to write. In this example, this song randomly played when I opened my Poetry Mix on Spotify. The songs I listen to are honestly never a discreet social commentary on the subject I'm writing about. It's just pure happenstance.

The Collective Wheel

What is the word
Who has the idea
Needed to change
Wanting to save
Us all
Pulling us out
Of this place
We got stuck
When we let
Idiots behind
The collective wheel
Drunk on power
Unable to steer
Refusing to see
What was clearly ahead
So, we hit it
And kept going
But only got this far
And it's painfully clear
We're not moving
All that much further
Until better heads
Fix what's broken
Take the wheel
And move us forward

        March 19, 2024
        Lenox, Massachusetts

Written while listening to "Savoir Faire" by Beth Ditto.

March

Tuning Fork

The steady sound
Rhythmically ringing
Is due to
The tuning fork
Feeding me
Audible spaghetti
Wound tightly

    March 19, 2024
    Lenox, Massachusetts

Written while listening to "Beautiful Life" by Gui Boratto and Luciana Villanova.

Small Potatoes

I can't grow as a person
If I remain content
Only eating small potatoes
At some point
I need to set my sights
On something bigger
And rise to the occasion
Becoming exactly what
I know I can be

                March 31, 2024
                Lenox, Massachusetts

Written while listening to "Vanille Fraise" by L'Imperatrice.

March

Orange Cat Tail On My Keyboard

It's hard to type
When there's
A swishing
Twitching
Super fluffy
Orange cat tail
On my keyboard
Covering the keys
Almost entirely
Actively trying
To distract me
From doing
This thing I do
Directing me
To give attention
To the tail's owner

    March 31, 2024
    Lenox, Massachusetts

Written while listening to "Blue Jeans – RAC Mix" by Lana Del Rey & RAC.

Returning The Favor

The old people have it wrong
When they repeatedly say
That young people don't want to work
Of course they want to work
They are standing up for themselves
And refusing to allow themselves
To be constantly used and abused
For the sake of excessive profit
Like previous generations did
Since there's no such thing
As anything resembling corporate loyalty,
They're simply returning the favor

>	March 31, 2024
>	Lenox, Massachusetts

Written while listening to "Je Suis Le Vent" by Working For A Nuclear Free City.

March

The High Holy Day

Time to celebrate
The high holy day
When chocolate, eggs,
And cute bunnies
Conspired and got together
Making sweet treats
Resembling themselves
Often married with
Peanut butter
And sometimes hidden
As a fun game for children

        March 31, 2024
        Lenox, Massachusetts

Hoppy Easter!

Written while listening to "Cornflake Girl" by Tori Amos. I haven't heard this song in years.

Something Found

Something found
Within a line
Within a photo
Where?
It doesn't matter
Only that it
Inspired
Movement
And action
On the part
Of the see-er
Whose life
Has now
Been changed
From sitting
To doing

                March 31, 2024
                Lenox, Massachusetts

Written while listening to "Neon Dad" by Holy Fuck.

March

Distant Squirrel

Out there
More than
A hundred feet away
On the thinning end
Of a reedy branch
Was the silhouetted outline
Of a distant squirrel
Cautiously approaching
The dangerously narrowing
Upper branch of a tree
Swinging and dipping
Under its tiny weight
As it kept trying
To move forward
But I didn't see
Where it could possibly go
There were no other
Branches nearby
To safely jump to
And then it seemed
To lose its footing
And swung upside down
Hanging onto the underside
For more than a moment
Until it righted itself
And briefly, thankfully, retreating
Back to the thicker,
More stable side of things
Until, for some reason,
It turned around again
Heading for the thin,
Unsupportive end
Like a tiny dark ball
With a smaller elongated bit
Its fluffy tail
Always obediently following
The flittering whims

Of its tiny rodent mind

After watching this for a while
I allowed myself a second or two
To glance back at my computer screen
And when I looked back up
The squirrel was gone
Nowhere on the branch
Or those nearby
Or winding down the trunk
Or sitting on a higher perch
Leaving me worried
That it went too far
And fell the fifty feet
To the ground
Which is something
I'd rather not think about
So, instead I'm imagining
It retreated to the trunk
And went further up
And is safely inside
Its comfy, cozy squirrel home
Getting ready to put an acorn pie
Into the oven, settling down
To watch some Netflix or something
Just as all squirrels like to do

>March 31, 2024
>Lenox, Massachusetts

Still, I'm probably not going to be venturing out into the far backyard anytime soon, just in case. I don't want to chance seeing a squished squirrel.

Or, risk running into the bear that's been visiting my front porch every night this past week.

March

Written while listening to "Opal – Four Tet Remix" by BICEP & Four Tet.

The Comfortable In-Between

APRIL

Spring Is Sneaky

Spring is sneaky
Spring is stealthy
One day everything
Within sight
Is sticks and dead
And on the next
There's a green tint
You can't directly see
But it blurs
And it hides
The edges
Which slowly encroach
From the heart
Of the forest
To the edges
Of the houses
At which point
It's nearly summer

    April 13, 2024
    Lenox, Massachusetts

Just the other day it was nothing but sticks in the woods behind my house. Now, the buds are starting to come out and nature is starting to get dressed.

Written while listening to "Regret" by New Order.

April

Polite Dryer

Today I had the chance
To use a polite dryer
Which gave me
Everything I reached for
In exact and proper order
Organized by clothing type
First out of the door
Was all of my long-sleeved
Button-up shirts
One after another
Then, my work pants
Followed by my undershirts
And then my underwear
With only my socks remaining
I removed and folded the last
The entire time, this dryer
Thoroughly impressing me
With its organizational skills
Whether it be by coincidence
Or some kind of fated moment
It was weird and wonderful
And a real joy to experience

    April 13, 2024
    Lenox, Massachusetts

True story!

Written while listening to "It's Time To Wake Up 2023" by La Femme.

Will AI Replace Me

Will AI replace me?
Probably
But what can I do
Likely nothing
So, I just keep at it
Doing what I do
Until I can do it no more
At which point
AI will win
But only because
It has the potential
To always outlast me

        April 13, 2024
        Lenox, Massachusetts

Written while listening to "The Birth And Death Of The Day" by Explosions In The Sky.

April

The Echoing Edge

The echoing edge
Of the arrow's blade
Signaling a chance
For a real change
That can only display
As one of two ways
A hit or a miss
With both parties
Wanting vastly
Different results

        April 13, 2024
        Lenox, Massachusetts

Written while listening to "The Mystery Zone" by Spoon.

What May Land On The Paper

Writing is dedication
Knowing that what
May land on the paper
Might not get read
By anyone anywhere and
Being totally okay with that
Because it's not about
The fame or the wealth
But about that
Deeply seated need
To get the thoughts out
Whether planned or not

    April 13, 2024
    Lenox, Massachusetts

Written while listening to "South Carolina" by John Linnell.

April

Like The Page

The start of something
Is unorganized
And often faltering
Like the Page
New to the wonder of it all
Eyes in the sky
Taking it all in
Unaware of the things
That absolutely can and will
Trip you up repeatedly
Until you have the experience
To look down and around
Taking in a bit of everything
Ensuring that falling
Will soon be a thing of the past

                April 13, 2024
                Lenox, Massachusetts

Written while listening to "Release The Squid (Box 6)" by The Deathray Davies.

Going To Be Great

I always think
The interior view
Of a car wash
Working around me
Is going to be
So spectacular
To the point
Where I always have
My camera ready
And I take pictures
Thinking they're
Going to be great
But
They never are
They aren't even
Interesting
In an abstract way
Just pale-colored suds
On the windshield
For a moment
Until they're washed off
And that's it
Nothing remarkable
Not a bit noteworthy
Despite me
Always thinking otherwise

        April 26, 2024
        Provincetown, Massachusetts

I was thinking about how I washed and vacuumed the car yesterday before our trip to Cape Cod and that got me thinking about this.

Written while listening to "One Thing" by Peter and Kerry.

April

I Think It Was The Cucumber

Overheard on the street
At night and in passing
As one man was relaying
A story to another
And ended up saying:
"Something happened…
 I think it was the cucumber."
A snippet that left me wanting
Needing, craving, *more*
Information on what transpired
Getting this middle bit
With no beginning
And no ending
Is making my mind
Do incredible gymnastics
Making up situations
To fill in the blanks
That have been cruelly inflicted
On my randomly passing ears

        April 26, 2024
        Provincetown, Massachusetts

True story.

Written while listening to "Transition To…" by Matt Berry.

Did The Math

A chilly April evening
Walking down the street
In this touristy town
Before the tourists arrived
When a pedicab passed by
And the driver must have clearly
Sized us up and did the math
Before asking if we wanted a ride
Maybe he was up for the challenge
Or he was overconfident
In his pedaling abilities
Because if it were me
On his bicycle seat
I would have passed us by

    April 27, 2024
    Provincetown, Massachusetts

Written while listening to "Ride" by The Dandy Warhols.

This is one of those weird coincidences where I'm writing about a pedicab driver asking if we wanted a ride when my playlist randomly gave me a song called "Ride." So weird.

April

At The Click

The space between
The wanting
And the getting
Can be impossibly distant
Or freakishly instantly close
Like ingredients tossed
Into a blender
Does it have power?
No?
Then nothing happens
At the click
Yes?
Then you won't even hear
The click
Over the high-intensity blending
Overpowering everything
Blasting all senses with a fury
Previously never known

        April 27, 2024
        Provincetown, Massachusetts

Written while listening to "Whatever You Like – Single Version" by Anya Marina.

This is one of those instances where the song completely shaped and inspired the poem. I just heard and wrote.

Demanding Attention

Today I was driving
And was stuck behind
A truck featuring
Bumper stickers
Demanding attention
For their big cause:
Motorcycles
With one insulting:
"Watch out for motorcycles, dumbass"
(The comma was added by me
 Because it needed the punctuation)
With another informing:
"Motorcycles are everywhere!"
And the other
Also insulting the reader, while
Pleading for respect, by saying,
"Respect for bikers!"
With a cartoon bike rider
Giving the middle finger
To the reader
Leaving me wondering
What exactly are they trying
To accomplish here
Are they wanting
Non-motorcycles
To be aware
And be safe around them?
Or,
Are they trying to
Be all "tough guy"
And offend
While at the same time
Being like
"Please don't run me over"
I honestly don't get
The mixed messages
They're presenting

April

April 30, 2024
Lenox, Massachusetts

I still don't get it. It would be helpful if people put a weensy bit of thought into their declarative statements they choose to stick to their vehicles.

Written while listening to "Isobel" by Bjork.

Fifty

Today is
Half a century
Of me
Fifty years
Of life
Failing and
Succeeding
My way through
This time around
But now with the knowing
That the time left
Is rapidly diminishing
So, it's high time
To get my shit together
And get my ass in gear
So, when I finish
I can look back
And be happy with
What I've accomplished
And not be worried
About the mess I've left –
Pay that no mind
Because every life is messy
And populated with
Piles of things started
And never completed
So, let's hope
That I get organized
And leave a tidy footprint

April 30, 2024
Lenox, Massachusetts

Written while listening to "Florida!!!" by Taylor Swift on repeat.

April

The Comfortable In-Between

MAY

Spring Is Blooming

Spring is blooming
Color aplenty
Combined with
Vibrancy in motion
Surrounded by nothing
But various shades
Of the deepest emerald
Newly fresh and alive
Showing the world
How life is done right

                May 1, 2024
                Lenox, Massachusetts

Written while listening to "Juju" by Jobii.

May

Seventeen Years

Right now
Time is flying by
So…*too* quickly
But
When we look back
To the recently last
Seventeen years
It's been a real
Roller coaster
Of living,
Moving,
Experiencing
The ups and downs
The rights and lefts
The speedy bits
The slow turns
Totally *really* living
Stuffing ourselves
Completely silly
With everything
We can see
We can reach
That this big,
Awesome
Amazing life
Has on its shelves
Taking advantage
Of the moments
While they're here
In our grasp
Nearly every time
Making sure
By the time
This crazy ride ends
We can be happy
And confident
That we can say

We've *lived*
We've really lived
These lives we were given
And I'm so happy
To have you
Here by my side
The one who's made
This journey
So fun
Thank you
For these seventeen years
And let's keep going
For many more

        May 5, 2024
        Lenox, Massachusetts

Happy anniversary, Kari!

Written while listening to "Oh No Darling!" by Sarah Kinsley.

May

The Interrupters

The interrupters
Choosing to invade
Your personal space
With their small talk
Nothing but
Verbal word salad
Wilted and bad
Without a single
Interesting or
Redeeming quality
And once delivered
The onus is on you
To eat it up
And play the game
To seem polite
When a connection
In the most insipidly
Shallow way
Is not anything
You want
Or need
In this moment

    May 7, 2024
    Lenox, Massachusetts

When you're out and about, doing stuff, minding your own business and someone feels to need to start blathering at you about something that you don't care about – only because they can't deal with silence and have to fill it with an inane, one-sided conversation.

Written while listening to "Reckoner" by Radiohead.

Fun fact about Radiohead. Back in the 90s, when I was in college at UMass Amherst, and when Radiohead was *just* starting to get airplay for "Creep," I saw them open for Belly ("Feed The Tree") at the Student Union Ballroom. In college, I didn't have much money, so I would get into concerts by working security. Because I was a tall, big guy, they always put me in "pit" security (the people standing behind a barrier that separated the crowd in front of us, and the stage with the band behind us). We were the ones who had to push people back who tried to climb up on stage. During Radiohead's set, Thom Yorke just barely missed whacking me in the head with his guitar at one point. Later, someone in the audience threw a shoe at him and they almost walked off stage as a result.

Note: Hahahahaha! Two songs later on my Poetry Mix on Spotify was the song "Black Swan" by Thom Yorke, which I just added to the "2024 Poetry Collection" mix just because coincidences are funny and weird.

May

Ghost Ticks

Despite our yard
Having been
Recently mowed
Nice and short
And only spending
Twenty minutes outside
Now, hours later
I'm feeling
The creeping crawling
Very real feeling
Of things moving
On my arms and legs
But, when I look
Nothing's there
Other than the
Ghost ticks
That only live
In my mind
Clinging tightly
To the notion
Of me being
Out in the yard

        May 7, 2024
        Lenox, Massachusetts

Written while listening to "Little Talks" by Of Monsters And Men.

The Act Of Stumbling

The act of stumbling
The moment of thinking
That falling
Might be a real possibility
Is often much worse
Than the landing
Than the hurting
The action of anticipating
All the probabilities
During the fraction
Of an actual moment
Is the real problem

        May 12, 2024
        Lenox, Massachusetts

Written while listening to "Need Your Love" by Tennis.

May

Fade And Fall

The passing
From one flower
To another
Is tracking
The passing
Of time
As the daffodils
Fade and fall
While tulips
Reign supreme
And roses
Are warming up
But even those
Will be gone
As the seasons
Move forward
Since nothing
Ever stays
The same

        May 12, 2024
        Lenox, Massachusetts

Written while listening to "The Fall" by Rhye.

Solely And Only

Ignoring the advice
Of the version of you
That was only an hour ago
Eschewing the notes
Damning the reasons
Moving forward
Solely and only
By the seat of your pants
Is absolutely
A-okay
Once in a while
However
That being said
It's probably
Not a general rule
By which
To live one's life
If you want it
To last somewhat
Longer than
A lesser amount

    May 12, 2024
    Lenox, Massachusetts

Written while listening to "To The Top" by Murray A. Lightburn.

May

Bundled-Up Notions

Gearing up for the hot times
Meaning leaving behind
The bundled-up notions
Of being comfortable
With temperature
Of being comfortable
With over-exposure
Leading to keeping
Up with the times
And preparedness
For all situations

        May 12, 2024
        Lenox, Massachusetts

Written while listening to "Summertime Cowboy" by Husky Rescue.

This evening, I wanted to do something different by writing as quickly as possible to whatever song came on – with the extra challenge of needing to finish writing before the song finished. Whatever popped into my mind, fueled 100% by the song, was what I wrote.

Resonance

Resonance
Vibrating within
Escaping
The confines
Impacting
The surrounding
Entities with energy
Making change
As a direct result
Making a difference
In the decisions
Made by others
Completely due
To what you
Chose to do

                May 12, 2024
                Lenox, Massachusetts

Written while listening to "Montreal" by Kaki King.

Coincidental sidenote: The song "Resonance" by Home came on a few songs later in my playlist (so I added it to the 2024 Poetry Mix playlist).

May

If Not, Then Oops

The act of falling
Is not inherently
A bad or terrible thing
As long as what
Caused the fall
Is actually worth
The potential outcome
If so, then great
If not, then oops

        May 12, 2024
        Lenox, Massachusetts

Written while listening to "Your Life In The End" by Prince Rama.

Sparking

Sparking
Leading to
Flaring
An explosive
Bursting
Infinitely expanding
The situation
From nothing
To all-consuming
Everything
In a matter of moments
Leaving the participants
Wondering
If survival
Will actually be
Possible
Or if they will be
Happily surrendering
To the burning
They ignited

    May 12, 2024
    Lenox, Massachusetts

Written while listening to "Moonchild" by Iron Maiden.

May

They Want

Trapped by the
Association
By those chosen
To surround you
By your own
Flawed judgement
That didn't do
Due diligence
That didn't do
The required checks
To make sure
These people here
Are actually in it
Because they care
And not because
They want
Something
They want
Everything
They know
You have
But now
It's too late
Because they're in
And they're here
Doing as they please
And the situation
Is beyond stopping
Because you let
Them in
Because you let
It happen

           May 12, 2024
           Lenox, Massachusetts

The Comfortable In-Between

Written while listening to "All My Friends" by LCD Soundsystem.

This one was a pretty long song (almost eight minutes) so it was pretty easy to write while the song played.

And thus ends my "write quickly to the music" challenge for the evening. Thank you.

May

With Each Application

Driving past places
I've applied at
So many locations
Rejected from
With a consistency
And a frequency
That seems almost
Automatic
That's becoming
Traumatic
To keep doing this
Over and over
Getting the same
Result
Again and again
So difficult
To keep on going
But I must
So I continue applying
Despite absolutely knowing
The inevitable ending
That's soon coming
With each application

                May 18, 2024
                Lenox, Massachusetts

Written while listening to "Strange Overtones" (David Byrne & Brian Eno cover) by We Barbarians.

A Portland Song

The major markers of my life
Have always been
Where I've lived
The physical place
A new start
In a new city
Supplying the setting
The background for me
During that time
Since I seemed
To have moved
Every few years
The music I listened to
What was going on
In my work,
In my life
Is mentally sorted
By geographic location
So, a certain song, for me
Might be a "Portland song"
Or, I identify a memory,
Or a taste, or a smell
With some other place
Like Huntsville, Manchester,
Boston, or Edmonds
While others rely
On a calendar
To mark the passing of time,
For the frequently moving
The answer lies in
Where I was living

    May 18, 2024
    Lenox, Massachusetts

May

This concept seems so perfectly normal to me that when I try to put myself in the place of someone who's only lived in one area and never moved, and then try to think back to a certain period of life it makes my brain say *ERROR ERROR*. I just can't conceptualize what that must be like. I mean, the longest I've ever lived in one place since I've been an adult was the four years I lived in Portland, Oregon (I really miss it there, but I wouldn't move back). I've just always marked the passage of time by my location.

Written while listening to "Suburban War" by Arcade Fire.

What The Cheese Log Tells Me

What the cheese log tells me
About the economy
About manufacturing
About corporate profit
And what I'm willing to spend
Is a startling education
Knowing the wanting
But completely stopping
When seeing the price
So ridiculously too much
For something not needed
That is only just a want
A cheesy log-shaped
Almond-sliver covered want
That I won't be buying today

May 18, 2024
Lenox, Massachusetts

Almost every time I'm at the supermarket, I see cheese logs (or, cheese balls), and think, "Ooh! I haven't had one in a while. I think I'll get one…" then I see they're over $8, when they used to be $4, and I'm like "There's no way in hell I'm spending $8 for a cheese log." Corporate greed is sometimes too much to take.

Written while listening to "Plenty" by Sarah McLachlan.

May

Past The Here

Life, while young,
Seemed so bright
And everlasting
Like nothing
Would ever change
Or, if it did,
It would all be kept
Securely in stride
As any thought
Of ageing or the future
Seemed so completely
Way off in the distance
Like it was too far away
To even remotely consider
But now I'm here
Actually, past the here
That the past me thought of
When thinking about
Potential and possible futures
And I'm in a place
And in a time
That would have never
Ever been considered
As something that could be
An actual possibility
And yet, here I am

          May 18, 2024
          Lenox, Massachusetts

Written while listening to "Rudderless" by The Lemonheads.

No Sign Of Sine

A line of light
Straight, flat
No variation
No sign of sine
No blips
No boops
Nothing of note

A smooth brain
Devoid of folds
Minimal activity
Supporting life

A canvas, blank
Without paint
Or work, or marks
Hung as complete

A huge empty room
Painted blinding white
No shadows, no art,
No furniture, no anything
Just empty and devoid
Of character, of variation
No complexities
Just boring emptiness

An old Caucasian man
Wearing a red hat
Flying political flags
From their truck
And on their house
Wanting to deny
To others
What they enjoy
While wheezing a single note
Heard and repeated

May

With no variation
With no exception
Incapable of changing
Impossible to attempt
Any critical thinking
They are just happy
Being completely
One-dimensional
In every respect,
Despite not having
Any to give

        May 25, 2024
        Lenox, Massachusetts

Written while listening to "Can I Play With Madness" by Iron Maiden.

The Comfortable In-Between

You Can't Coddle

You can't coddle
The fascists and
The racists
Otherwise
They get brave
And emboldened
And begin to think
Their wrong way
Is the right way
As their echo chamber,
Loud and screaming,
Makes them believe
They are the majority
When they are nothing
But a fraction of a minority
Of a tenth of a percentage
Dying out, alone and afraid

    May 25, 2024
    Lenox, Massachusetts

Please be part of the solution and stamp it out whenever it rears its hateful head.

Written while listening to "Never Mess With Sunday" by Yppah.

May

Keto For Vengeance

Glancing quickly
Over books on a shelf
When one title
Catches my eye
Makes me look back
And re-read it
And relax a bit
After realizing
It was
Keto For Vegetarians
And not
Keto For Vengeance

    May 25, 2024
    Lenox, Massachusetts

Hahahaha. True story.

Written while listening to "Feel Good Inc." (Gorillaz cover) by Filous and LissA.

Distill And Define

Imagine being defined
By a job you had
For only one year
And proudly bragging
Constantly displaying
The hats, the stickers
Flags, shirts, anything
Showing the logos
Wanting, demanding
Attention for this thing
For decades to come
Despite reality that this was
Barely done, so briefly
Hating every moment
While immersed in it
Yet always wearing it
On their sleeves
Choosing to distill
And define
An entire life
By this one thing
A life simply without
Any complexities
Or interests
Or anything outside
Of this one thing

        May 25, 2024
        Lenox, Massachusetts

Of the four poems I wrote tonight, I started by writing this one, but I wasn't sure if I was going to add to it or change it. I thought more and started to change it, but that ended up becoming "No Sign Of Sine."

Written while listening to "White, Discussion" by Live.

May

The Comfortable In-Between

JUNE

The Comfortable In-Between

Punk Shoe Wool

Being on time
Repeatedly
Consistently
But not really
Spoken phonetically
Uttered quickly
With a difference
Gets you to the place
Where the phrase
Punk shoe wool
Gets you there
On time

    June 1, 2024
    Lenox, Massachusetts

Written while listening to "Let It Burn" by Le Blonde.

This is probably in my top five most listened to songs of the past few years.

June

The Scribbled Thrumming

The scribbled thrumming
Messy and incoherent
Distorted and disjointed
Completing the background
Repeating and echoing
Acting as if we asked for this
Rather than the staticky surround
We've learned to tune out
In the course of daily existence

>June 1, 2024
>Lenox, Massachusetts

Last night I went to Amherst, Massachusetts to see Buffalo Tom in concert at The Drake. In my first semester, freshman year, at UMass, I joined UPC, the student-run production company that brought concerts to campus. I wanted to be exposed to new music and see more live music, but I couldn't afford to pay to get into concerts. UPC allowed me to work the shows, get in for free, and get a free tee shirt. Because of my size, they always had me do pit security, so I was one of the three people who stood facing the crowd, while behind a barricade that separated them from the stage and the band immediately behind me. My very first concert I saw doing this was Buffalo Tom. I liked them so much that I went out and bought their *Birdbrain* cd the next day. According to my concert spreadsheet, this was the fourth time I've seen them (1992, 1994, 2004, and 2024).

Anyway, all of this to say that when I was watching Buffalo Tom play last night, their dirty, distorted, gritty guitar playing made the phrase "the scribbled thrumming" pop into my mind, so I wrote it down. Today, I picked it up and did something with it.

Written while listening to "I Need A Connection" by Jane Weaver.

The Comfortable In-Between

Why Is My Neighbor Mowing Completely Naked

Why is my neighbor
Mowing completely naked
At least that's what
I totally thought
When I first saw him
Round the corner
Maybe it was the light
Or the shadows
Playing tricks with my eyes
But it took a few seconds
To realize he was wearing
A flesh-colored shirt
And similar shorts
While happily zooming around
On his ride-on mower

                June 1, 2024
                Lenox, Massachusetts

This happened, just now.

Written while listening to "Na Na Song" by The Jon Johns.

June

The Touch Removed

The touch removed
The pressure –
Expected, wanted,
Fully used to, was now gone
Instantly, the lack thereof
Is immediately felt
The impression left on the skin
Slowly rising,
Attempting, resuming
To the state prior
To the craved compression,
The contact was gone
Yet, the heat remained
But was undeniably cooling
Each degree was a loss
That was not acceptable
Yet another digit counting against
The wishes, in addition
To the moments
Slipping away
Separating back then
A few seconds ago
To the near
And far future
Where
The touch
Is not replaced

        June 8, 2024
        Lenox, Massachusetts

Written while listening to "Yellow Light" by Of Monsters And Men.

The Comfortable In-Between

I saw this band in 2012 when I lived in Vermont. They were just starting to explode in popularity with their debut full album, *My Head Is An Animal*. Prior to seeing them, I always skipped this song, which was the last one on the album. It was too slow and "boring" in my mind.

When I saw them, they played it and, holy wow, it absolutely blew me away. The repetition part that takes up about half the song was so powerful and to be in a crowd where everyone was singing along really changed my opinion of the song. Now, it's one of my favorites on this album and I often will listen to just this one song on repeat.

June

The Reason To Loop Back

The connection
Isn't just part of it
It is the entirety
It is the purpose
The cause
Of the return
The reason
To loop back
To this place
Again and again
From way back then
To the forward future
Feeling, experiencing
Whole new lives
Different circumstances
Dissimilar goals
In the end, perfection
Doesn't matter at all
Life is sloppy and dirty
As we ricochet our way
Through this dense mess

        June 8, 2024
        Lenox, Massachusetts

Written while listening to "Sæglópur" by Sigur Rós.

Funny that two songs in a row were from Icelandic bands.

The Breadcrumbs Of Existence

The writing needs to take prevalence
Over most anything else
The leaving of little creations
Dotting the path back
Along the entirety of my past
The breadcrumbs of existence
So next time I'm here
I can more easily
Find my way
And get on track
Faster, quicker
The mode of the vehicle
Doesn't matter as much
As doing, creating,
Generating momentum
Being propelled along
Because once the words
Are arranged on the screen
And once the art
Is marked on the canvas
A statement is made
And a body of work
Is slowly being built
A brick here
And a beam there
Will build up to become
A house you can
One day
Live in

    June 8, 2024
    Lenox, Massachusetts

Written while listening to "Style (Taylor's Version)" by Taylor Swift.

June

Note: I also happen to be wearing a Taylor Swift tour shirt.

Additional note: I, unfortunately, did not see Taylor on tour. I just have the shirt.

Static Cling

Static cling
Makes me sing
Every time
I do the laundry
Little wee lightning
Quickly shocking
The tiny stabbing
With the crackling
Which is only cool
When it's dark
And you can see the light

    June 8, 2024
    Lenox, Massachusetts

Written while listening to "Turn Tail" by Young Knives.

Also, Welton the cat (full name: Sir Welton Fluffytail), came by wanting pets and flopped on the keyboard. His contribution is: "4+++"

June

Gentle Rain

Gentle rain
Starting quietly
So faint
That you think
It might be
A breeze
But it's clearly
Raining
With the addition
Of the duet
Of wind
Rustling
The trees
And the leaves
Giving a freshness
To the breeze
As it passes by
Kind of like Febreze
But less chemically –
A more naturally
Occurring version
That is better
And fresher
And making you want
To stay here
In this moment
Doing nothing more than
Staring into the dark,
Listening, and breathing

          June 8, 2024
          Lenox, Massachusetts

This is happening right now. I have the big slider door that goes outside to the back porch open (the screen door is closed so cats don't go out and bugs and bears don't come in) and it just started raining.

Written while listening to "Ascent" by GoGo Penguin.

June

The Approaching Thunder

Light filtering through
The approaching thunder
Deep-carrot-orange
With ash-gray edging
Canvassed on bright blue
With charcoal slate
Quickly moving in

        June 14, 2024
        Lenox, Massachusetts

The sunset was unreal tonight as a thunderstorm moved in.

Written while listening to "Take Out" by Brian Witzig.

The Creative Inside

The creative inside
Waking up
Shaking off
The imposed sleep
Unfairly thrust upon me
By life's "must do" list
Which absolutely
Does not understand
That want I want to do
Ranks infinitely higher
Than this day-to-day stuff

                June 14, 2024
                Lenox, Massachusetts

Written while listening to "Contact" by Daft Punk.

June

Scam Texts

Scam texts
Lack satisfaction
Where I want to be
The type to engage
To waste their time
To outwit these fools
But, at the same time
I don't know what
They're capable of
Nor do I want to get
Put on some sort of list
Saying I'm to be targeted
By all of their other
Scammer co-workers
So, I do the boring
And sensible thing
By blocking them
And reporting
As spam

    June 14, 2024
    Lenox, Massachusetts

Written while listening to "More Important Than Michael Jordan" by Pretty Lights.

A Perpetual Motion Machine

The process of building a thing
Is hard when you're just starting
When you don't have plans
When you're just winging it
And you have no idea
What shape things will take
But, as you go,
And place block upon block
The general idea
Will start to form
And that's when
The spark happens
And momentum
Starts to take over
Fueling the movement
Inspiring yourself
Becoming nothing short of
A perpetual motion machine
Of creative energy

    June 14, 2024
    Lenox, Massachusetts

Written while listening to "Chicago" by Sufjan Stevens.

June

This Is Where I Am

This is where I am
This is what I'm doing
Which is exactly
Where I should be
And what I should be doing

    June 14, 2024
    Lenox, Massachusetts

Sometimes I need to remind myself of this because all the time I'm thinking "Yeah, I'm here doing this *but,* I *NEED* to be over there doing that." It's okay to be happy where I am.

Written while listening to "Choir To The Wild" by Tinlicker.

Getting Started

Getting started
To get going
On the thing
I've been
Imagining
Wanting
Planning
For far too long
Because now
I'm through
The weeds
And the forest
And it appears to be
Smooth sailing ahead

                June 14, 2024
                Lenox, Massachusetts

Written while listening to "Car Fiction" by Echobelly.

Equaling This Place

Thinking about
My place here
In this spot
In location
In time
On this planet
In this Universe
And seeing how
It all fits together
How it seems like
I've riding on
A conveyer belt
A walkway
Moving me along
In a very curved,
Circuitous path
But with a purpose
For every turn
With a reason
For every interaction
No matter how small
There've been things
To glean, to learn
From everything
So, when I meditate
And rise above
The forest I'm in
The perspective
Plainly provides
The clarity I see
As the connections
Between
Each point
In this life
Becomes so comically
Visible and obvious
As the coincidences

The Comfortable In-Between

Pile up impossibly tall
That it's a wonder
I hadn't noticed
The pattern,
Or put two and two
Together
(Times a thousand)
Equaling
This place
Where I am now
And the direction
I'm moving in

      June 16, 2024
      Lenox, Massachusetts

Written while listening to "Clarity" by Hammock.

Sometimes I sit down to write with nothing planned, but when I start a song playing, the words just come out of my fingers onto the keyboard. It's like this song wrote the poem, not me. (Note: this song has no words, it's an instrumental.)

She Knows It All

Despite knowing nothing
She knows it all
Simply by observing
On her daily walks
And deeply speculating.
The other day
This Boomer busybody,
From up the road a ways,
Cornered me
On my way to the mailbox
Wanting to talk
About the house
Across the street
That's been for sale
For almost a year
But seems to have
Unusual activity
According to Karen,
(Her name and profession)
Wealthy parents
Bought the house
For their adult son
To live in
But also so they
(The parents)
Can stay there
When they want
To go to Tanglewood
Or other cultural events
Despite her version
Not making a lick of sense
Because the house
Is still for sale
Because being directly
Across the street
We see when showings happen
And she, does not

The Comfortable In-Between

And we saw when
Trucks appeared
To haul stuff out
Like carpeting
And furniture
So, I nodded politely
And indicated
That I needed
To get my mail
And get going
Without sharing
That, to us,
It seems like
The people she thinks
Are the new owners
Are actually workers
Staying in the house
As they renovate it
Which I don't mind
Sharing with you
Because you don't know
The house
The people
Or the situation
As you have
No skin in the game
As opposed to
Keeping what we know
From Karen
Because the terrible cycle
Of rumors and speculation
Needs to stop somewhere
Like right here and now

June 16, 2024
Lenox, Massachusetts

Buzz off, Karen.

June

Written while listening to "Think Twice" by Ralph Myerz and the Herren Band.

Grilling View

What a nice and perfect day
Standing outside on my deck
Grilling tonight's dinner
Nice except for the neighbor
Vacuuming his car
Which is weirdly loud
And my watch confirms this
By saying the decibels
Are a bit much at the moment,
I look up to see a contrail above
Leaving me wondering
Where this plane is going
Which an app conveniently tells me:
Reykjavik, Iceland
To Baltimore, Maryland
Which seems like
A strange direct flight,
Then I hear some nice birdsong
Which I don't recognize
So, out comes another app
Which, after listening,
Says a junco and a robin,
And, as I put the burgers on,
I wonder how long
And what temperature
So, I look it up
And, like everything else,
Here in my grilling view,
I now know the answer
Like an all-knowing master

      June 22, 2024
      Lenox, Massachusetts

True story.

June

Written while listening to "Killer in the Streets" by The Ravonettes.

A Stunning Inundation

Today, it rained
An absolute downpour
Buckets upon buckets
A stunning inundation
Probably only slightly short
Of actually being torrential
Because I'm trying to be
Factual here and not
Embellishing for the reader
Because reporting matters
When cats and dogs
Are falling down around me

    June 22, 2024
    Lenox, Massachusetts

Today it rained a surprising amount for a solid 10 to 15 minutes. It was crazy-go-nuts. It made me think of when I used to live in Portland, Oregon, yes it rained a lot there, but it was such a misty light rain and never much more than that. I think the whole time I lived there, I only heard thunder once. The people who live there didn't even own umbrellas, they all just had hooded raincoats.

Written while listening to "Fuckin 'n' Rollin" by Phantastic Ferniture. (That's how they spell it – I don't make up the band names.)

June

Solstice Waning

Two days past
Meaning that now
We're in the phase of
Solstice waning
The build up
Is freshly past done
Like a pre-heating oven
We're still in for the worst
But each night
From here on out
Will be a little longer
As we barrel toward fall
While most everyone
Is focused solely on summer
Uncaring and unaware
Of the diminishing details
Indiscernible at this moment
But growing steadily daily
Working on the ending
Of this summer season
Just as it is beginning

    June 22, 2024
    Lenox, Massachusetts

Every year I always worry how I'll eventually end up writing the exact same thing I do every year about the solstice, but different. Every year, I end up doing it (by not reading what I've written in past years – I could totally be re-writing the same poem. Who knows!).

Written while listening to "Vad Hände Med Dem?" by The Brian Jonestown Massacre.

Survey Worried

I had to call a company
About a thing
And the person
Was actually really helpful
And she asked me
To take the survey
After the call
Which I wanted to
Because she was great
But
I absolutely wasn't
Paying attention
In the slightest
When the automated voice
Was giving instructions
On what number response
Indicated how happy or mad
I was with the service
That I received
So, when it asked how helpful
The employee was to my needs
I stared wide-eyed at my phone
Because I honestly didn't know
What number was the best
Was it one? Was it five?
I hit five
Sending me into a panic
What if it was out of ten?
And all this dithering
Made me miss the next question
So, I pressed nine –
Not knowing if I could enter ten
And, for the last one
I entered ten, again not knowing
But stressed and worrying
That I might have inadvertently
Given this very nice woman

June

A bad score
Which could hurt her
When I only wanted
To help her

        June 22, 2024
        Lenox, Massachusetts

Written while listening to "To You I Bestow" by Mundy.

The Hero

I keep telling myself
I don't want to write
About what's going on
In this country
At the moment
Because it's too dark
Too bleak
And we've already
Been here once before
But with each self-promise
Not to go there
I, of course, go there
Because the worry
Is foremost on my mind
And the hero
We've all placed
Our trust in
Turned out to be
As good as nothing
Unable to stop
What's coming

                June 28, 2024
                Lenox, Massachusetts

Written while listening to "Human Behaviour" by Bjork.

The Arid Landscape

The arid landscape
Of a place
I can no longer support
Because we end up voting
Every time we spend money
And that's not something
I want to vote for anymore
Is still someplace I hope
That someday I can
Visit once again
To see the red rock mountains
Forged by forces
Over millions of years
Be the screen
The sunset movie
Is played upon
Lighting up
Highlighting
Brightening
Giving flourishes
To every nook
To all the rocks
Making up the hills
Playing their part
For our benefit

    June 28, 2024
    Lenox, Massachusetts

Written while listening to "Caroline" by Concrete Blonde.

Note: my 2024 Poetry Mix playlist says I already used this song this year, but that's okay. It still inspired this poem.

Regret

To wonder
What's my reason
To be in this place
To occupy this life
To do what I'm doing
Is normal
Whereas
To avoid
Thinking about it
To sidestep
Reflecting on
This important subject
Is a cowardly thing
Done by those
Who fear the answer
Done by those
Who intimately know
Regret

                June 29, 2024
                Lenox, Massachusetts

Written while listening to "Regret" by New Order.

June

The Brave Faithful

A steady rain
Falling down,
And on, those
Gathered for
The concert
Picnics prepared
And carried in
Filling with water
Blankets on the grass
Soaked through
Cup holders
On the top of
Wheeled coolers
Filled to the brim
With rainwater,
The attendees
(The brave faithful)
Wearing raincoats,
Covered in tarps,
Or soaked to the bone
Enjoying the space
Left by the skipped
And the show
Still playing before them
Clearly muted
But still playing

           June 29, 2024
           Lenox, Massachusetts

All day today it's been raining. Steadily, but not heavily. In my town is Tanglewood, the summer home of the Boston Symphony Orchestra and the Boston Pops. They also have a lot of popular artists play there as well. Last night it was Jon Baptiste. Tomorrow it's Brandi Carlisle. Next month, I have tickets to see Beck. Tonight, it's Trey Anastasio with the Boston Pops. I've never

The Comfortable In-Between

listened to Trey's solo music, but I am aware that he's in Phish. Back in the 90s, when I worked summers managing the store at the local Boy Scout camp (Chesterfield Scout Reservation – long since closed), there was a guy on staff who was NUTS about Phish and he played their *A Picture Of Nectar* album non-stop. I probably haven't listened to it in maybe 25 years, but tonight, after seeing that his show was getting a good soaking, I put on that album. Meh, it's just kind of okay. That's not me being snobby about music…according to Spotify, I listen to over 2,500 different bands every year. I generously fill my ears with a *lot* of different music, but I'm just not interested in what Phish is selling.

Anyway, this poem is thinking about what it must be like for those watching the show tonight.

Written while listening to "Cavern" by Phish.

June

Suddenly Became Popular Somehow

Today
While waiting
For my appointment
At the local Warby Parker
I was a bit surprised to hear
One of the songs I recently found
Last summer, playing on the speaker
Of the store's hip musical playlist
Making me mouth the words
And happily tap my foot
While wondering if this
Is something that's
Suddenly become
Popular somehow
In the recent past
Without my
Knowing

        June 29, 2024
        Lenox, Massachusetts

Written while listening to "Edge Of Town" by Middle Kids. This was the song I heard today.

Also, as I started writing, I noticed that each line was slightly longer than the previous one, so I kept up that pattern until about the middle, when I brought it back in.

Also, also, the "local" Warby Parker is an hour away in Albany.

Also, also, also, I was not very adventurous. I ordered the same pair of glasses that I currently have. Last year, I got a "normal" pair and a "crazy" pair that was bigger and the frames were a clear bright blue. I never wear the blue ones (they're a bit "statementy" for my tastes). I did get order new sunglasses, which are nice.

Doing Double Duty

Art can be anything
Or nearly so
With its life depending
On the views of the viewer
And if they're drawn into
Or repelled by
By the art in question
With the best of it all
Doing double duty
By accomplishing
Both simultaneously

           June 29, 2024
           Lenox, Massachusetts

Written while listening to "Right Here, Right Now" by Fatboy Slim.

June

The Comfortable In-Between

JULY

Sporadic Explosions

Sporadic explosions
Piercing the night
Scarring the calm
Making no sense
Because it's raining
Probably only happening
Because it's the Saturday
After the Fourth of July
And the disruptors
With the illegal fireworks
Feel the need to shoot them off
Only because it's a Saturday night
And they're drunk so why not?
Despite the rain chucking down
Soaking their pyrotechnics
Hopefully rendering them
Completely wet and useless

    July 6, 2024
    Lenox, Massachusetts

Written while listening to "Down I-5" by case/lang/veirs. This is such a beautiful song. I feel bad that it came up randomly while I was writing this poem about idiots blowing shit up…this song deserves a more appropriate and fitting poem.

July

I Started Something New

I started something new
A new-to-me thing
That I hope to do
At least once a day
Maybe I'll keep it up,
Maybe I'll get better
Or, maybe I won't
But I won't know
Unless I at least try

        July 6, 2024
        Lenox, Massachusetts

I started doing a simple and fun art project. I'm hoping that one year from now I'll have 365 small digital art pieces. They're similar to the quirky and eccentric style of David Shrigley. I'm really enjoying it.

Written while listening to "Open" by The Cure.

The Comfortable In-Between

Feel The Pull

Is it possible
To feel the pull
To two cities
In opposite directions
At the exact same time?
As one city
Well known to me
Where I used to live
Takes me by the hand
Showing me memories
Of what I used to love
About where I lived
A continuous slideshow
Playing in my mind
While another city
A place I've been to
Only one time
Is taking my other hand
And pulling me
Across an ocean
To a metropolis
Filled with promise
And new adventures
Around every corner
And I'm here
Stuck in the middle
While Portland
And London
Pull me apart
Leaving not a lot left
Where my roots
Are currently planted

        July 6, 2024
        Lenox, Massachusetts

July

I've been experiencing a bit of homesickness for Portland (Oregon) lately. I know things are different there now than when I lived there ten years ago, and I would never move back, but I still feel the pull, nonetheless. That, combined with a deep desire to return to London, has been pulling me in two very different directions. I know these are just "wants" and not "needs" and the feelings will subside. I mean, I *really* planted roots here in Lenox and I'm not interested or intending to move again.

Written while listening to "Here Come The Waterworks" by Scout.

A New Phase Of Me

Is it bad
Is it wrong
That I see this thing
I used to be in
And think
It looks
Small, subpar,
Not worth it and
A bit amateurish
Like it's a thing
That isn't worth
My time, energy,
Or even the
Minimal effort
To whip off
A little something
Maybe it's a sign
That I'm growing
Beyond this thing
And moving into
A new phase of me

    July 6, 2024
    Lenox, Massachusetts

Written while listening to "Radio" by Lana Del Rey.

July

I Simply Won't

All I want to do
Is that new thing
And nothing else
Because it is
Wholly exciting
And the notion
Of me pacing
Myself or facing
Applying some
Kind of brakes
Feels crazy insane
And I simply won't
Do anything
To slow this down

    July 6, 2024
    Lenox, Massachusetts

Written while listening to "Tom Courtenay" by Yo La Tengo.

The Sun Will Still Rise

Even though, right now,
It feels like this can't happen
But the Earth will still rotate
The sun will still rise
Tomorrow and every day
The birds will wake
So insanely early
To go out and about
Doing their bird things
Oblivious of what
Is consuming
Is ruining us
In our minds
As we worry
Needlessly
About the future
And about humanity
We have to pause,
Breathe,
And know
That the world
Will still continue
That the collective
Issues that trouble
Us as a country
Mean nothing
To nature
To the world
To the Universe
And, this too,
Will pass

        July 6, 2024
        Lenox, Massachusetts

July

I can't forget to pause and breathe. No matter how bad things look, look at nature still doing its nature stuff and try to relax.

Written while listening to "Circle" by Sarah McLachlan.

A Rancid Patchouli Way

The intense smell
Of grandmas gone by
Too sickly sweet
In a rancid patchouli way
Bragging about
How blessed they are
Discussing all their
Medical problems
Trying to one-up
One another
As they pass
Their remining time
Playing cards
With just a hint
Of gambling

                      July 9, 2024
                      Lenox, Massachusetts

Written while listening to "Don't Talk About You" by Geowulf.

July

And Naturally, Expansion

Opening
The mind
Causes
The filling,
And naturally,
Expansion
To happen
Regardless
Of intention

        July 9, 2024
        Lenox, Massachusetts

Written while listening to "Changes" by Sugar.

Something Sustainable

Can I do it?
Just be open
To whatever
Pops up in
My mind
Just from
Listening to
A random song
Maybe it's
Possible
But honestly
I don't know
If it's something
Sustainable
Which I guess
Is depending
On momentum
As long as
A great start
Is something
That's happened
I would assume
That you can
Just keep going
Despite not knowing
Where any of this
Is ultimately heading
Which is why
At this moment
I'm actually stopping
Sorry

                    July 9, 2024
                    Lenox, Massachusetts

Written while listening to "Rim Shack" by Letters To Cleo.

July

In February of 1995, I saw Letters To Cleo at Pearl Street Nightclub in Northampton, Massachusetts (with Gravel Pit and Gigolo Aunts opening). It was a great show, and I've always liked their *Aurora Gory Alice* album. I should listen to it more.

The Sparkle Of Fireflies

An hour or so ago
I set up my GoPro
In hopes of recording
The sparkle of fireflies
Blinking and fluttering
All around in the humidity
Making the night magical
With all their twinkling
During their brief appearance
Giving us something to remember
On an otherwise forgettable
Latently hot Tuesday night

                    July 9, 2024
                    Lenox, Massachusetts

I don't know what a group of fireflies is. Hold on, let me look it up. It is a "sparkle" of fireflies. That's a great descriptor. I originally had "flock of fireflies," so I'm going to change it because "sparkle" is so much better.

July

Was Anything Really Missed?

The ticket
For the show
To which
I did not go
An experience
Seemingly wasted
An opportunity
To see a singer
I sorta knew
But not quite
At least not
Anything recent
So, thinking
Back on it all
Was anything
Really missed?
Instead of going
Out and fighting
Traffic and dealing
With finding parking
We enjoyed the couch
And watching something
Really interesting
On the YouTubes
While eating cake
And petting cats
Making it a really nice night
Despite missing the concert
Or, maybe because
Of our missing the concert

        July 25, 2024
        Lenox, Massachusetts

Two nights ago we ended up staying in instead of going to Tanglewood to see Beck perform with the Boston Pops. We had tickets, but earlier in the day, Kari was feeling pretty lousy. She did end up feeling better by the evening, so we could have gone, but honestly, we just didn't feel like going.

Written while listening to "Whiteout Conditions" by The New Pornographers.

The Perfect Response

"We are not going back"
Is the perfect response
Where we make a stand
Against the barked command
Meant to line the pockets
Of a single man
While selling hats
And a lifestyle
Stupidly sloganed
In a nonsensical way

        July 25, 2024
        Lenox, Massachusetts

Written while listening to "God Is A Bullet – Live" by Concrete Blonde.

While The Eyes

The beats are still coming
While the eyes are not closing
Despite the pillow comforting
And the lateness of the hour
Bordering on being early
Of a new day just dawning
Outside where the world
Is awakening freshly
With the breaking light

    July 31, 2024
    Lenox, Massachusetts

Written while listening to "Insomniac Olympics" by Blockhead.

July

Brevity

Brevity
Providing the conditions
The exacting framework
Dictating the road taken
Upon which you choose
To drive

        July 31, 2024
        Lenox, Massachusetts

Written while listening to "Synchronize" by Discodeine and Jarvis Cocker.

Bananas

Someday soon
When bananas
Are extinct
You'll tell
Your children
How cheap
They used to be
And
They won't
Believe you

                July 31, 2024
                Lenox, Massachusetts

Written while listening to "In The End" by Think Of England.

July

Wary Of The Bear

The other night
We heard banging
Coming from outside
And as I turned on
The bright porch light
Stepping into the night
Just in time to see
The large dark shape
Of a pretty huge bear
Trotting away
Towards the woods
And I surveyed
The damage done:
The latch to the shed
(A small one
 only holding
 the trash bin)
Half ripped off
The door open
The large bin
Tipped over
The garbage
Strewn about
Trash everywhere.
Wary of the bear's
Potential and
Eventual return
I grabbed a shovel
And re-filled the bin
Returning it to the shed
Trying to get the door
Back to being latched
But not being successful
We thought it was
Good enough for tonight
But we were wrong
Because it returned

The Comfortable In-Between

And resumed doing
Its bear job of looking
For the yummy food
We had thrown away
So, pans in hands
We smacked them
With metal spoons
Making a racket
Retreating the bear
And this time
We asked The Google
What we should do
And we learned
They hate the smell
Of bleach so very much
So, we doused a shirt
In too much bleach
And hung it on the door
Of the somewhat broken
Little trash shed
And piled half a dozen
Very heavy bags
Of potting soil against
The partly open door
And topped it off
With the shovel
(Just in case)
And that,
Thankfully,
Worked

        July 31, 2024
        Lenox, Massachusetts

Written while listening to "The Suburbs" by Arcade Fire.

July

The Comfortable In-Between

AUGUST

The Bottle Of You

Sadness distilled
Under the process
Of taking memories
(Only the most
 heart-wrenching will do)
And subjecting them
To time and pressure
And constant re-thinking
(Endless re-thinking)
Where the edges of details
Blur and fade away
Ensuring only the absolute
Hardest moments to face
Remain in the charred
And blackened
Elemental crucible
Before being shaken up
Exposed to gravity,
Anxiety, density,
And more difficulty
Then finally,
Attractively,
Pre-packaged in
The bottle of you
Expertly advertised
Completely misdirected
As to the actual contents
Leaving the buyer
Completely unaware
Until they pop the top
And release
Everything
That's been
Bottled up
Making it all
Explode
Everywhere

August

Extinguishing
The good times
That had been had
Up until that moment

    August 8, 2024
    Lenox, Massachusetts

Written while listening to "Smile Like You Mean It" by The Killers and "Information" by Eliot Sumner.

Click Click

Click click
Of the keys
Sending the
Information
Click click
Go the cogs
Seamlessly
Intertwining
Inside minds
Seeing words
Understanding
The connection
Between this
And everything

        August 15, 2024
        Lenox, Massachusetts

Written while listening to "We'll Bring You Down" by Winterpills.

August

Rudderless

Rudderless
Like that old song
From the mid-90s
Just drifting about
Aimlessly
As if there's
Any other way
To be drifting
Because to do so
With intent
Would be,
Essentially, lollygagging
Or, otherwise
It would be
Simply a lie
To say you
Intended to do this
Because you don't get here
To this place you're in
Through careful planning
And rigorous intent

    August 15, 2024
    Lenox, Massachusetts

Written while listening to "I Wanna Be Adored" by The Raveonettes.

All The Nouns Left Behind

The past is often portrayed
Like a road or a river
Implying that it's possible
To turn around and go back
To the people, places, and things –
All the nouns left behind,
But that's not at all accurate
As the past is more of a swamp
With the things you knew
Resting somewhere down
Deep in the murky depths
Beyond sight
Beyond reach
Completely inaccessible
Except for the memories
Softly fading, and dulling
In the mind
But that's entirely okay
Because what's here
Right now
Is the so much better
Inevitable conclusion
That may not have been expected,
But is, thankfully,
Where you ended up

                    August 15, 2024
                    Lenox, Massachusetts

Written while listening to "Take My Hand" by Matt Berry. I know this is the theme for the silly show, *Toast Of London*, but dang, this is also one of my favorite, and most listened to songs.

August

Directions

Directions
Are important
Knowing
Where to go
What to do
Is essential
To moving
Forward and
Advancing
Without which
You could be
Wandering
Aimlessly
In the kitchen
While baking
That cake, or
Completely lost
On a highway
Hours off track
With no idea
How to get back

        August 15, 2024
        Lenox, Massachusetts

The cake directions are the most important ones.

Written while listening to "Southern Point" by Grizzly Bear.

A Fresh Resetting

A fresh resetting
Has happened
Which has actually
Brought hope
Where there was none
Brought joy
When we thought
We'd not see it again
Brought energy
When we needed it most
Inspiring us all
To rise up
And take action
To make sure
We, as a society,
Can continue
To continue
As we've known

        August 15, 2024
        Lenox, Massachusetts

A couple of weeks ago we happened to be driving within sight of the Colonial Theater in Pittsfield when Vice President Harris was there at a fundraiser with James Taylor and Yo Yo Ma. Seeing the thousands of people outside in the blocked off street out front was really wonderful.

Written while listening to "My Only Swerving" by El Ten Eleven.

August

Stripped Of His Soapbox Moment

In the supermarket
Looking, trying to find
The shredded cheese
In the style I wanted
When a man to my left
Loudly proclaimed,
"Unbelievable!"
In the annoying way
Of someone wanting
To start a conversation
With someone.
I was hoping *not me*
So, I ignored his bait
While I contemplated
Various types of cheese
When the man repeated,
"Unbelievable!"
This time, even louder
And clearly in my direction
I looked over to see a man
Probably in his late sixties
Glaring intently at me
Pointing hard, like he was
Trying to burst a balloon
That was refusing to pop
His finger stabbing toward
A display of Land O' Lakes
His words, dripping with hate
"The price of butter
 is out of control!"
With his words released
He continued to stare at me
While his finger kept jabbing
The air in front of the butter
Like he was broken
And stuck in a loop
Waiting for me to respond

The Comfortable In-Between

Just over and over
Staring harder
Pointing harsher
Waiting for a response
I would not give him
And this continued for
A purposely and
Fully awkward minute
With me not responding
Not even in the slightest
No cracks of laughter
No words of wisdom
My eyes locked on his with
Absolutely nothing from me
A stone cold blank slate
Not wanting to waste
A single syllable on him
Or engage this man
In any way
I was not going to fall
Into his pre-planned rant
About the economy
Or the government
He picked up from
A Facebook meme
Or some AM radio program
When I had had enough
I tossed my cheese
In my cart,
Turned around
And left the aisle
The way I came
Leaving him alone,
Dumfounded,
And, most importantly,
Stripped of his soapbox moment

        August 25, 2024
        Lenox, Massachusetts

August

True story. Happened at the Big Y (or, "Grand Pourquoi" as Kari and I call it) in Lee, Massachusetts last week.

Written while listening to "Summer" by Buffalo Tom.

Pop Ups

Website
Acting normal
Until the
Pop ups
Appeared
Popping up
No
Click
Fuck off
Click click
Go away
Click click click
Goodbye

            August 25, 2024
            Lenox, Massachusetts

Written while listening to "Elle ne t'aime pas" by La Femme.

August

The Position

Once again
Not getting
The position
I applied for
I'm overqualified for
I can do easily
And perfectly
While at the same time
Helping out
With everything else
They could ever need
Because once again
They went with
Another candidate
Just like the other times
At the other places
For the other jobs
I applied for
Being passed over
Ninety-something times
So far
Has been demoralizing
And degrading
As I head out on an errand
And go past a dozen places
In my three-mile drive
I've been rejected from
I try to block them out
Pretend they don't exist
Which means my drive
Anywhere in the area
Is full of buildings
And businesses
That are invisible
And are no longer there
Each one deadening me
A little more each time

The Comfortable In-Between

All of which makes me
Wonder what this
Amazing thing
The Universe has in store for me –
The reason why
I haven't been getting
Any of these jobs
Because the perfect thing
Is yet to come
But diggity dang
It sure is taking
Its sweet-ass time
In getting here

        August 25, 2024
        Lenox, Massachusetts

This last rejection was especially tough because it was a perfect fit for me, and I had two amazing rounds of interviews for it. I *knew* I had it…until I didn't.

Written while listening to "Thinking Of You" by Kesha.

August

Reset Refocus Regroup

Following the setback
Getting knocked down
Yet again
Bruised, with the fight
Completely knocked out
And just lying there
While giving up
Seems to be
The reasonable solution
After so many times
But you need a little time
Separating you
From the bruising source
Time to
Reset
Refocus
Regroup
Because maybe
Just maybe
The direction
You repeatedly
Attack from
Is the wrong way
To be going about it
Maybe a little time
And some planning
Along with a new direction
Can finally lead you
Not just to victory
But to an entirely
New level
New place
You hadn't even considered

August 25, 2024
Lenox, Massachusetts

The Comfortable In-Between

Written while listening to "Fireplace" by Lost In The Trees.

August

The Comfortable In-Between

SEPTEMBER

Stickers

The sticker on the pickup
In the olde-timey
Hard-to-read font
Boldly saying
"PITT CREW"
As a "witty" way
To try and say
They have a group
Of people who are
All from Pittsfield
And who all have
The same sticker
Affixed to their cars
As if their inherent need
To try and convince others
That they have friends
Who also aren't afraid
Of lowering the value
Of their trucks and cars
By putting stickers
On their vehicles

    September 1, 2024
    Lenox, Massachusetts

Written while listening to "Our Motto" by Dear Leader.

September

The Best Summer Ever

The retirees who use this area
As their summer playground
To escape from the heat
The dreadful humid summer
Of their terrible Florida towns
To their second homes
Nestled in our hills here
Where they drive poorly
Clogging roads and stores
Griping all the while
About how this area
Is not what it used to be
While buying tickets
For the performances
At this, that, or the other
Complaining how
It's not like how it was
So many decades ago
Grumbling about how
It's too busy everywhere
There are too many people
And how they liked it better
When this was a hidden gem
And then, like it began,
The summer ended
And they flood southward
Where they preen and brag
To their canasta and mahjong groups
About their amazing and perfect
Summer in the Berkshires
And all the wonderful things
They did and what a dream it was
And how it's too bad
They couldn't have come
To have experienced
What they did
And how they missed

The Comfortable In-Between

The best summer ever

        September 1, 2024
        Lenox, Massachusetts

Written while listening to "The Edges Are No Longer Parallel" by Morrissey.

September

The Routine Of Creation

The routine of creation
Is a building one
Starting with a foundation
Full of cracks
And poorly poured
But the more you build
You fill the cracks
Making it stronger
While it grows higher
With each level better
Until, years later,
You're surprised
And full of pride
At what you've created

    September 2, 2024
    Lenox, Massachusetts

Written while listening to "Bad Thing" by Miya Folick.

Struttin' Their Puffy Stuffs

Out for an evening drive
At the turn of the seasons
Freshly left the summer months
While just beginning the cooler
As the sun goes from
Just above
To
Just below
The curvy, hilly horizon line
While I was on my short drive
Changing the landscape
From perfectly-lit
Golden glow all over
Anything and everything
To mild shadows deepening
While all eyes are
Up on the skies
At the pink and orange clouds
Struttin' their puffy stuffs
While jumping over the hills
That are just beyond the lake
Whose shores are full of those
Taking a quiet moment to fully
Appreciate the inspirational beauty
Put together for us to enjoy

    September 2, 2024
    Lenox, Massachusetts

True story. We spent the day reorganizing and working on the rooms where we'd just piled lots of boxes two years ago when we bought this house, and never got around to unpacking/doing something with and felt like being very lazy for dinner, so I went out to McDonald's in Lee and picked up dinner. On my way down, the sun was still up, although, just barely, and on my way back home, it had set and was making the sky look beautiful and

September

colorful. It was the kind of scene that I wished I could have been able to take a picture of, but since I was driving, I had to settle for appreciating the moment and trying to re-tell it later when I had a chance to write.

I'm always so afraid of not fully appreciating the swing seasons when I'm in them; you blink and they're gone. From summer with sunsets after 9pm to winter with darkness at 4:30pm before you can even sneeze.

I had intended on calling this one "Inspirational Beauty" but after writing the "struttin' their puffy stuffs" line, I quickly changed my mind.

Written while listening to "Cirrus" by Bonobo.

The Nights Too Cool

The air condition-less days
Of the past two weeks
Have finally yielded to
The nights too cool
To leave the windows open
For fear of it being too cold
To make the thermostats click
Bringing them back from the dead
And making the house smell like
The pungency of hotly burning dust

    September 2, 2024
    Lenox, Massachusetts

Written while listening to "Young & Unafraid" by The Moth & The Flame

September

I Hit An Age

My eyebrows used to be
Ideally thick
In just the right places
While at the same time
Perfectly shaped
As if sculpted by a god
And they still are
Mostly
Because it seems
I hit an age
Where errant hairs,
That have always
Been well behaved,
Decided to act out
And grow out
At weird angles,
Lengths, and spirals
Making a mess
That's getting
Out of control
And now needs
Constant attention
And trimming
To keep it looking
Somewhat normal
Which is something
I don't much care for

September 2, 2024
Lenox, Massachusetts

Written while listening to "Total Fascination" by Pretty Lights.

Normally, my poetry is directly inspired by the music I listen to, but the four poems I wrote tonight just happened to be on in the background and didn't really inspire any words. It was just a bunch of great songs to listen to while I wrote.

September

In The Waiting Room

We'll call you by your number
They said repeatedly
To the woman
Who kept trying
To cut the line
Despite seeing everybody
Sitting there, waiting
In the waiting room
Until comprehension
Somehow creeped in
And she took a number,
Sitting with the rest of us

        September 10, 2024
        Lenox, Massachusetts

Written while listening to "Home (feat. Saavan)" by Mount Dreams.

Within Reach

Tapping into
The energy
Swirling and
Hanging around
Is easy once
You get the gist
Of how it works
The knowing
It's right there
Within reach
The connecting
Quickly followed by
The initial feeling
Building and swelling
An energy empowering
Sometimes sharp and pointed
Other times mellow and soft
But still powerful, nonetheless
Every type is different
Depending on what you seek
Depending on what you need

     September 10, 2024
     Lenox, Massachusetts

Written while listening to "Infinite Dreams" by Iron Maiden.

September

Lifting Up

Judge a person
A place or a thing
And determine
Whether it
Or its energy is
Dragging down
Or lifting up
If, the former,
Cut it loose
And let it fall
Far and away
Never to pull
You down again;
If, the latter,
Embrace it and
Surround yourself
With as much
Of that energy
As you possibly
Can find, letting it
Lift you upward
To new places
Never considered

> September 15, 2024
> Lenox, Massachusetts

I just love YouTube so much. We spent a while this evening watching videos by different artists shopping for their art supplies. It was inspiring.

Written while listening to "Pacific Theme" by Broken Social Scene.

Steadfastly Refusing To Comply

Completely ignoring
Common sense and
Rational thinking
Instead substituting
Entirely false notions
Based in nothing
But incorrect feelings
Factually proven wrong
Again, and again, and again –
The irrationality angers me
And diminishes hope for hope
For those choosing to die on this hill
Thank goodness the new generation
Is using their collective voice
To stand up to the previous ones,
Steadfastly refusing to comply

    September 15, 2024
    Lenox, Massachusetts

Written while listening to "Sæglópur" by Sigur Rós.

September

A Grinning Sideways Smile

The nearly empty waiting room
Of the local urgent care office
Seeing the man who walked in
And immediately leans with elbows
Resting fully on the counter
With his face against the glass
Leaning in and looming over
With his shaggy face bristles
Pressing into the clear barrier
The poor intake employee
Probably leaning back away
But at least she could not see
The view I had from this angle
As the top half of his ass crack
Gave me a grinning sideways smile
As the beltless pants slid enough
To put his worst asset on display

              September 15, 2024
              Pittsfield, Massachusetts

Oh, Pittsfield.

Written while listening to "Something's Always Wrong" by Toad The Wet Sprocket.

It Still Feels Too Early

It still *feels* too early
For us to be discussing
The impending autumn
Even as the foliage
Continually drops
All around me
Despite the calendar
Also agreeing
With the leaves
That we're nearly there
With one foot firmly
In the pumpkin spice season
But, for me, it seems
Like we should be in July

        September 15, 2024
        Lenox, Massachusetts

Written while listening to "Take A Bow" by Matt Berry.

September

Notably Apart

The song
That's the
Outlier,
The one
That stands
Notably
Apart from
The catalog
Is the one
That really
Most clicks
And resonates
So completely
With me

        September 15, 2024
        Lenox, Massachusetts

Written while listening to "That Time" by Regina Spektor.

The Eroding Slope

Wondering what
The next step is
When it seems like
The footfalls below
Are completely gone
As the remnants still here
Try hard to navigate
The eroding slope
Precariously perched
Above the angry waves
Thrashing the land,
Removing the options,
Of where I hoped
I could next stand
While trying to plan
For the future when
The present is
Wholly uncertain
Is really degrading
The last of my optimism

    September 15, 2024
    Lenox, Massachusetts

Written while listening to "Experience" by Ludovico Einaudi.

September

The Act Of Creation

The act of creation
Is the lasting impression
The enduring mark separating
The completely forgotten from
The occasionally remembered

    September 15, 2024
    Lenox, Massachusetts

Written while listening to "Mexican Moon" by Concrete Blonde.

Reinterpreted Beauty

Continually explaining
Textually, visually,
The creative retelling
Of the scene seen
And needing to be
Translated to another
Format, medium,
As a means to convey
Reinterpreted beauty

        September 15, 2024
        Lenox, Massachusetts

Written while listening to "And Stars, Ringed" by Blue Sky Black Death. This is one of my favorite and most listened to songs.

September

When The Lightning Flows

When the lightning flows
So harmoniously
So continuously
So wonderfully
So predictably
So reliably
So dreamy
You let it continue,
No matter the hour,
And you bottle that shit

                September 15, 2024
                Lenox, Massachusetts

Written while listening to "Grand Union" by Arthur Beatrice.

Emotional Paint

Why tonight?
Is it something
About anguish
That squishes
A part of the mind
Putting pressure
On the parts
Forcing creativity
To spray out
In all directions
Covering the canvases
With emotional paint
Well, it's clearly
Nothing pretty
That's for sure
But I guess it worked
A weird kind of magic
Allowing me to write
A prolific amount
In an otherwise
Ordinary evening

> September 15, 2024
> Lenox, Massachusetts

I wrote ten poems tonight. There was probably four or five times I was like, "Okay, that's it for tonight!" and then another great song would come on, or another idea would pop in my head and I just kept going.

Written while listening to "Modern Man" by Arcade Fire.

September

Knowing When To Write

Knowing what to write
Is completely unimportant
Compared to
Knowing when to write
If the timing works out
The words will flow

>September 17, 2024
>Lenox, Massachusetts

Written while listening to "Deadly Valentine" by Charlotte Gainsbourg.

An Attempt To Sway The Business

Words spoken
Like a confidant,
A secret salesman
In an attempt
To sway the business
In his direction –
Instead, making me
Inherently distrust him
And want another opinion

                  September 17, 2024
                  Lenox, Massachusetts

I brought my car into the dealership for an oil change and I ended up leaving with an expensive list that recommended new brakes and all new tires on my four-year old car. No. Tomorrow I'm getting a second opinion.

Written while listening to "The Hop" by Radio Citizen.

September

The Comfortable In-Between

OCTOBER

Portobello Road

A neat idea
In a place
Immortalized
By a beloved movie
So, we stayed
And we visited
Notting Hill
At a place
Called The Lost Poet
Which would have been
Mildly apt, but it wasn't
Not in the least
Because I know where
I am and am cognizant
Of my location at all times,
But here we were
Setting out in the morning
From the bottom to the top
Of Portobello Road
On Saturday, market day,
Which was interesting
To experience in real life
But holy hell
It was wall-to-wall people
As tens of thousands of us
Slowly moved along the road
As somewhat junky stalls
Passed by on either side
While my mind fretted
The entire time
That we were surrounded
Completely by pickpockets
Every few seconds I patted
My wallet and my phone
Snugged deeply in their pockets
Just to make sure they were there
And not walking off

October

In a different direction
With someone else
Intent on stripping them
Of any and all value

>October 5, 2024
>The Lost Poet guest house – Notting Hill, London

I'm glad we went and experienced it, but I would not go again. The stuff in the stalls was not worth the constant paranoia about pickpockets stealing our wallets/phones/etc.

Written while listening to "Femininomenon" by Chappell Roan and "Night Mail" by Public Service Broadcasting.

The Comfortable In-Between

A Worst Class Experience

Booked the train
From London to Bath
Decided for this direction
To spring for upgraded seats
And got first class tickets
Which the railroad billed as
A luxury experience
And the only way to travel
But but but
Our train was cancelled
So, they smooshed us all on
The next one going in the same direction
Which was overloaded to the point
Where hundreds didn't have seats
And the class division broke down
Giving everyone a worst class experience
With so many having to stand in the aisle
For the hour and a half ride
Yes, we were technically in the first class
But we had many asses sitting
On the table between us
To which there was no remedy
Because of how overfull the train was

    October 6, 2024
    The Queensberry Hotel – Bath, Somerset, England

Written while listening to Brutal by Olivia Rodrigo.

Note: The train ride was not "Brutal" by any stretch of the imagination, it was fine for us because we actually got to sit – it just so happens that this song was playing on my playlist while I was writing this poem.

October

Separated By The Ha-Ha

Just a few blocks away
From our fun, weird hotel
Is the Royal Circus
Which is so neat
But is not the subject
Of what I want to write about
So, I move on, around a third
Then along Brock Street
Two more blocks
When my view opens up
Expansive greenery
Ahead and to my left
A large park used by
Local dog owners
Throwing frisbees
And enjoying this place
Separated by the ha-ha
As a way to say
All of you may enjoy
This lower portion
But this upper part
Separated by this small wall
Visible only to you
But invisible to us
Who live up here
In the Royal Crescent
Who only see
An infinity pool
But made of grass –
A perfectly maintained lawn
The height of which
Helps to hide all of you
Frolicking down below
Past the ha-ha
Which is what we say
Every time we look down
In your direction

The Comfortable In-Between

October 6, 2024
The Queensberry Hotel – Bath, Somerset, England

Written while listening to "Memories" by Strabe.

October

Bath

Immersed in a bath while surrounded by
And looking at Bath
The distant green field hills
Dotted with black and white cows
The stone homes in the middle distance
Lumped and grouped together
In a hodge-podge way
The famous landmarks close by
Like the thousand-year-old Abbey
And the Roman Baths
And the Pulteney Bridge
While I am relaxing on this tall rooftop
In near-hot tub temperatures
Watching the English birds fly by
And enjoying this special moment

                October 7, 2024
                The Queensberry Hotel – Bath, Somerset, England

Earlier this evening we went to the Thermae Spa, which was wonderful. We started out in the huge indoor pool area downstairs. This room had probably 40-foot-high ceilings and glass walls. Certain areas of the pool were bubbly like hot tubs, but not as hot. There was an actual current flowing through and you could just float on through it. We went upstairs to the spa rooms where they had things like saunas, infrared saunas, and this neat cold room. It was so foggy you couldn't see anything. There was a room-wide trough against the far wall that was full of shaved ice. You were supposed to take handfuls of ice and put it on your skin. Brr! Then we found lounging seats in a space-themed sauna room. It had pictures from NASA projected on the walls, as well as other blinking LEDs on the ceiling. After that, we went to the rooftop, which was a big rooftop pool (probably on the 6th floor) that overlooked all of Bath. It was a chilly late afternoon/early evening and it was so cool to be in this very warm pool and looking at things like the nearly 1,000 year-old Bath Abbey, the rest of the city (with every building made of the same colored stone), and the rolling green hills beyond. It was pretty magical.

Written while listening to Super Graphic Ultra Modern Girl by Chappell Roan.

October

A Repurposing

I like the times
When someone takes
Something really old
And modernizes it
In some neat, arty way
Even for a small time
It's like taking this thing
And giving it a repurposing
Which makes it freshly new
In a way our modern selves
Can better relate to
And more deeply appreciate

    October 7, 2024
    The Queensberry Hotel – Bath, Somerset, England

Tonight we went to the Shine On Luxmuralis light and sound display in the Bath Abbey. Basically, they had a very neat projection system that filled the entirety of the huge cathedral with amazing moving images and color based on the stained glass from the Abby. So neat that they did this. The Abby is beautiful already as it is (we went earlier in the day to see the inside), but this was like breathing a fresh, modern look to the inside of this 900-year-old space.

Written while listening to "At The Moment" by The Dead Milkmen.

English Country Roads

English Country Roads
Are scarily narrow
And are barely fit
For a wheelbarrow
And should be widened
Or, at least closed
Until this can be fixed

                October 8, 2024
                Stow-On-The-Wold, Gloucestershire, England

I can't tell you how scary it is to drive on the left for the very first time on such winding, wee roads that are only made for one car at a time.

Written while listening to "Deli" by Delorean.

October

Fleece Alley

When we leave the Airbnb
The only way to walk
To get to the center of town
Is to follow Fleece Alley
The same narrow way
That sheep were herded down
Hundreds of years ago
On their way to market
And so now, we follow
The same route on our way
To go get coffee and breakfast

        October 8, 2024
        Stow-On-The-Wold, Gloucestershire, England

Written while listening to "Some Girls Are Bigger Than Others" (Smiths cover) by Supergrass.

Model Village

A fascinating development
When the scale Model Village
Of your entire village
Is considerably more interesting
Than the village itself
Which is mostly made up of
Tourist trap shops
Set in a pretty backdrop

                      October 10, 2024
                      Bourton-On-The-Water, Gloucestershire, England

Written while listening to "Oh Mandy" by The Spinto Band.

October

What Does Matter

It doesn't matter when you last did
Something
What does matter is that you now have
The desire
To restart either where you left off or
Start again
Completely from scratch on square one
Leaving
The empty comfort that doing nothing provides
Stepping
Out on your own into uncharted goodness

                      October 10, 2024
                      Stow-On-The-Wold, Gloucestershire, England

Written while listening to "Krack" by Soul Wax.

The Comfortable In-Between

Seen The Aurora

If it weren't for
The drunk stumbling
Older woman
Floundering and swearing
In the private, fenced-in
Backyard of this Airbnb
I never would have
Gone outside, looked up,
And seen the aurora

>October 10, 2024
>Stow-On-The-Wold, Gloucestershire, England

True story! I heard the gate to Fleece Alley awkwardly bang open and a woman, who sounded to be in her 60s (?) was sputtering "fucking twat!" a few times and then the gate banged shut. A few minutes later, I ventured out to make sure she was gone, and that was when I looked up and saw the brilliant pink and green of the aurora filling the sky above. Thanks, sweary older lady!

Written while listening to "Twin Cinema" by The New Pornographers.

October

Scooch

While driving the too-narrow country roads
In the beautiful and scenic Cotswolds
I had to constantly remind myself
To drive on the left, on the left, on the left
While my wife sat in the passenger seat
Cringing as I kept veering to the left
To avoid the oncoming traffic
So, she came up with a signal
When she felt I was too close
To the left-side curb by saying,
"Scooch" every time I was over too far
While driving on the wrong side
In a car that was much bigger
Than what I was used to at home.
Oncoming car,
Veer slightly to safety
"Scooch"
Veer slight back to the center
And back into oncoming danger
Back and forth for miles and miles

    October 10, 2024
    Stow-On-The-Wold, Gloucestershire, England

I eventually, mostly got used to it, but holy wow, it was scary driving on those tiny roads. Weirdly, I did enjoy driving through rotaries going the "wrong" way.

You would not believe how many different ways I spelled "scooch" before I had to look up the correct way.

Written while listening to "Nothing Matters" by The Last Dinner Party.

Nothing But A Folly

After a drive
Then a walk
Confused by
The signs
And lack of
Direction
We ended up
At our intended
Destination
Broadway Tower
Definitely such
A pretty building
On top of a big hill
But in the end
It's still nothing
But a folly
Neat on the outside
Empty on the inside
Pretty to look at
But not much else
Going for it

        October 11, 2024
        Stow-On-The-Wold, Gloucestershire, England

I was really excited to go here because all of the pictures made it look so neat; and it was so impressive to look at. However, the signage there is terrible and we didn't know where to go or how to pay or do anything. We accidentally ended up walking up to a self-locking gate just as a group of people were leaving and we got in for free. It's cool, but honestly not worth the trip.

Written while listening to "From The Edge Of The Deep Green Sea (live)" by The Cure.

October

Driving On The Left

After a few days
It is amazing
How you get used to
Something brand new
Like, for instance,
Driving on the left
Which I thought would
Be beyond difficult
But was something
I did surprisingly well at
And now I'm left
With a real fear
That when I'm back home
I'll have trouble
Driving on the right

        October 12, 2024
        Stow-On-The-Wold, Gloucestershire, England

Written while listening to "Let It Go" by edapollo.

Back To London

Back to London
On the fast train
From Bath station
Zooming through
The countryside
Leaving behind
The Cotswolds
Where we wish
We had more time

                October 12, 2024
                On the GWV train from Bath to London, England

Written while listening to "Policy Of Truth" by Depeche Mode.

October

Walking Around Mayfair

Walking around Mayfair
Absolutely surrounded by
People who look and dress
Like supermodels
In the restaurant
On the sidewalk
Models everywhere
Or, for here,
Regular people
Who can afford
To look like models

        October 12, 2024
        The May Fair Hotel, London, England

Written while listening to "We Used To Be Friends" by The Dandy Warhols.

The Comfortable In-Between

The Best Way To Move

I love the tube
The underground
The best way to move
Myself around
This lovely town
Quickly, easily
Quietly, cheaply
Just hop on
And hold on
Because I'll be there
Where I want to be
In two shakes
Of a king's tail

                October 12, 2024
                The May Fair Hotel, London, England

Written while listening to "Utopia" by Digitalism.

October

Portraiture As The Focus

Entering the place where
The art on display is
Portraiture as the focus
Making me expand
My concept of art
In wonderful new ways
Based on the variation
And the concepts
From photography
To iconography
To true-to-life paintings
To the craziest shit
You can think of
From the expected
To the extremes
This place grabbed me
And pulled me
So many different ways

    October 13, 2024
    National Portrait Gallery, London, England

Written while listening to "End of World Party" by HÆLOS.

Dance Booth G

Sometimes you have to upgrade
The experience to better experience
The moment
Which is why we are here
In Dance Booth G
At ABBA Voyage
Where we can see
So much more
And move so much easier
Being so much freer
When the moment
When the music
Clicks just right
Like it does
For most of the entirety
Of this show

                    October 13, 2024
                    Pudding Mill Lane Station, London, England

Written while listening to "Dancing Queen" by ABBA.

October

I Am The Champion

By flukes
And coincidences
And mistakes
And shrewdness
And cleverness
And abilities
I am the champion

        October 14, 2024
        The May Fair Hotel, London, England

One of our favorite TV shows is *Taskmaster (UK version)*. It just so happened that when we were in London, they opened Taskmaster: The Live Experience, so we went. It was great! We had so much fun. In the end, I was the champion of our group (me, Kari, and an extended family of eight from Glasgow who we got lumped in with) and won a medal, and Kari was the "Best Of The Worst" and won a Taskmaster Best Of The Worst rubber ducky.

Written while listening to "Birdhouse In Your Soul (live)" by They Might Be Giants.

I Knew A Guy

Signed up for
And went out to
A lecture
While on holiday
At the V&A
Listening to an art person
Talk and ask questions to
The owner of a famous place
A restaurant known for its art
And each question was rebuffed
With a flippant reply
That very little to no
Actual planning went into the look
The feel, the design of the place
With answers like, "Eh, I knew a guy"
Or "I knew someone who knew someone"
Who was arty and did the design
Or curated the look
And had nothing to do with this guy
Up on stage, the owner
Who just owned the space
That others made into
A revolving and famous
Work of art

                October 14, 2024
                The May Fair Hotel, London, England

We saw this event listed on the V&A's website: Mourad Mazouz: The Artistry of Sketch hosted by Gianluca Longo. Last year we had afternoon tea at Sketch and it was a very neat experience. While the talk we attended tonight *was* interesting, hearing his responses was a bit disappointing.

Written while listening to "Experiment" by Shikimo.

October

The Tube

Seeing the signs
For the Tube station
Descending the stairs
From the street level
Keeping your mind on
The line you need
The direction you're going
While navigating the masses
Coming and going
While being hyper vigilant
About your wallet and phone –
Swipe in, through the gates,
Beeline to the correct line
Down an escalator
Around a corner
Through an archway
Down another escalator
Choose the right platform
Walk away from the crowds
To where it thins out
Look up at the sign
Saying how many minutes
Until the next train comes –
The hot rubbery smell
The dinging of the alert
And the announcement
Letting you know the train
Is now approaching
And to stand back
As the warm air whooshes in
Followed by the lights
And the sound
Of the metal tube
Speeding by and slowing down
With the squealing of metal
It stops while another dinging
Chimes as the doors open

The Comfortable In-Between

With dozens exiting each doorway
And the second it's clear
Dozens more entering and jockeying
For position, either on seats,
(If available) or for the best place
To stand, lean, or hold
In preparation for movement
When the voice of an actress
Lets us know the train is starting
We hold on the best way we know how
Based on subway physics
To limit our touching
Or bumping into someone else
As eyes dart up to the map
For this particular line
As everyone silently counts the stops
Until their destination
And while the miles of darkness
Pass on by, punctuated by
The occasional station
And re-shuffling of passengers
All eyes look at their phones
Or the advertisements
(The same ones seen on other trains)
Until the correct stop appears
And we prepare to go
When the doors open
Parting the waiting crowd
Minding the gap
Stepping out and then the moment
Where everyone stops and looks
For the black and yellow sign
Pointing WAY OUT
And then we all go that way
Around corners
Up stairs
Down hallways
Up escalators
Until we're in the lobby

October

And we re-swipe
Our cards to exit
Up one final flight of stairs
To enjoy the crisp cool blast
Of fresh outside air
Before we walk
Along the noisy and busy streets
In the direction
Of our chosen destination

           October 15, 2024
           The May Fair Hotel, London, England

Written while listening to "Understand Me Now" by Pretty Lights and "Night Mail" by Public Service Broadcasting.

Just A Quiet Space

Sitting in a park
With an amazing view
Just across the river
With a perfect view
Of Big Ben and Parliament
(No Funkadelic here)
Just a quiet space
Facing one of the most
Recognizable landmarks
On the entire planet
While having a lunch
From Tesco Express
And painting a picture
Of everything that I see
Making me thankful
For the opportunity
Of being here
And doing this
In this moment

    October 16, 2024
    St. Thomas' Riverside Garden, London, England

Written while listening to "Red Wine Supernova" by Chappell Roan.

October

The Speedboat Tour

If the description
Says those with neck,
Heart issues, or back
Should avoid this
Then probably
Everyone should
Give it a pass
All I wanted was to see
Views of the city
From the river
And I thought
The speedboat tour
Would be the same
As the others,
But a little faster
I did not count on
The insane driver
Putting the boat
Up to full speed
(Which I did not mind)
And then slamming it
Sideways into a skid
With the boat bouncing
Over the top of the water
On its side like a hammer
And then throwing the boat
Hard to the other side
Skipping like an upright stone
The wrong way over the surface
Terrified that if I didn't grip
The handlebar in front of me
Tightly enough I would fall out
Or worse
If the boat tipped too far
And our heads ripped off
Due to a miscalculation
By the rambunctious driver

The Comfortable In-Between

That didn't happen
But this terrifying ride
Continued like this
For a full fifteen minutes
Before returning level
And slowing down
When the tour part resumed
And I was left thinking
What if I had brought my mother
Onto this boat tour?
She would have easily
Lost her grip and been thrown out
Of the boat, or just plain died
Of a heart attack right there
But in the end, I enjoyed
The normal boat parts
And seeing the city
From the water
But never ever again
Will I get in their boats
And be taken
For such a terrible ride

October 16, 2024
The May Fair Hotel, London, England

Written while listening to "Tugena" by The Dead Milkmen.

October

Royal Warrant

I want to get
A Royal Warrant
For poetry
I could hang up
Here in my office
So, when the King,
Or Queen,
Wants to partake
Of some poetry
They simply
Have their people
Contact me
And I'll write some lines
And send them along
Making their days
Just a little bit better

        October 17, 2024
        The May Fair Hotel, London, England

Written while listening to "Dance Anthem of the 80's" by Regina Spektor.

The Comfortable In-Between

NOVEMBER

A Dudebro Chad

Walking past
A dudebro Chad
On the busy street
In a local touristy town
He's on the phone
Describing himself
To someone else:
"I'm just someone
 Who got bored
 Too quickly
 And didn't enjoy
 The scenery."
Yet, he is still here
Walking our streets
Enjoying our area
Pretending he isn't
To seem uninterested
And, somehow, cooler
In his smallish mind

>November 3, 2024
>Lenox, Massachusetts

This actually happened. I was walking on Railroad Street in Great Barrington recording a walkabout of the town for my YouTube channel when this doof walked by.

Written while listening to "Birdhouse In Your Soul" by They Might Be Giants.

November

A Tornado Of Color

A tornado of color
Sweeping through
Twisting up everything
And making it all new

        November 3, 2024
        Lenox, Massachusetts

I spent a surprisingly long time trying to make this into something very long and rhyming, but instead I deleted most of it and went with this simple bit.

Written while listening to "Millie Rode to Heaven on the Back of an Orca" by The Photographic.

Missing The Culture

We've been back for a few weeks
But I can't stop constantly thinking
About the trip we took to England
Not just the touristy parts
But the real-life bits
Where we're taking the Tube
Imagining that this is daily life
While popping into the M&S Express
To grab a few quick things
On my way home from work
Just that the routine aspects
Of life there are so much more
Appealing than over here
Where things are pretty much
Exactly the same but just
Slightly different in every way
Enough to make every interaction
Like a whole new experience

                November 3, 2024
                Lenox, Massachusetts

Written while listening to "The Last Cherry Blossom" by RudeManners.

November

A Portrait Faded

A portrait
Faded
A life
Dimmed
Dulled by time
Devoided
Of the spark
The light now
Barely there
Mostly diminished
But not aware
To realize
The amount
It has ebbed
Like a sunset's
Pale remains
Washed out
Well past twilight
Entirely surrounded
By darkness

        November 3, 2024
        Lenox, Massachusetts

It's jarring how early the sun sets now.

Written while listening to "Motherboard" by Daft Punk.

Hunker Mode

In order to survive
The next four years
We need to be in
Hunker mode
Where we
Avoid the news
Do our own thing
While not appearing
To be gay
Or trans
Or female
Or pregnant
Or non-white
Or non-Christian
Or born elsewhere
Or non-regressive
Or any of these
Or anything else
That's slightly different
From the recently made up
Social norms befitting
A racist, fascist,
Christian nationalist
And we'll be fine

                November 6, 2024
                Lenox, Massachusetts

Written while listening to "Ill Will" by D-A-D.

November

A Knowledge Of History

A knowledge of history
Has, unfortunately
Provided me
With a pretty good idea
Of how all of this
Will end up playing out
Which is why
I'm preparing for the worst
Mapping escape routes
Getting affairs in order
Planning, planning, planning
How to protect
My family from
The Low People who
Have made their intentions
And their methods
Painfully known

            November 12, 2024
            Lenox, Massachusetts

Written while listening to "Avril" by Burning Peacocks.

The End Result

The end result
Is that millions
Of people
Listened to
And believed
A pathological liar
And known idiot
Because he said
Something
In his constantly spewing
Completely indecipherable word salad
That appealed
To them

     November 12, 2024
     Lenox, Massachusetts

Written while listening to "The Sun" by The Naked And Famous.

November

Bullies Emboldened

Bullies emboldened
By the voting
Now come crawling
Out from under
Their rocks
Thinking being
A racist asshole bully
Is a-okay today
And approved
By anyone and everyone
From the elected one
On down to the neighbor
Who lives in the gutter
All trying to rule the roost
In their loud and boisterous way
Incorrect in their belief
That civility and respect
Have gone completely away

        November 12, 2024
        Lenox, Massachusetts

Written while listening to "Nights Off" by Siriusmo.

The Dark Cloud

The dark cloud
Up in the shy
Which looks like
An angry wolf
Mouth open
Backlit by the sun
Giving attention
To the teeth
Ready to chomp
Ready to grip
The target
Which is all of us

>November 12, 2024
>Lenox, Massachusetts

Written while listening to "Beach Break" by Julietta.

November

Maybe I Am In Control

How can you get motivated
When you've been
Completely demoralized
After spending the past week
In an excessively deep funk?
This is where I've been
This is where I am
This is where I was
Until I put on a song
Preferably one
That moves you
In a positive way
Ideally one
That has a rocking beat
And makes you want
To get up and do something
Which is what I just did
And now I feel a little better
Like maybe I am in control
A little more than I thought I was
Enough at least
To shake this off
And try to make a difference

    November 12, 2024
    Lenox, Massachusetts

Written while listening to "Physical Poetry" by Dramarama.

The Comfortable In-Between

The Smoothing Folds

Parroting versus thinking
Critically, which in this case
Is of critical importance
Because these days
What passes for thinking
Is merely digesting
The cud beaming
Into living rooms
By way of slanting news
Providing only
The daily talking points
Agreed upon in boardrooms
To be repeated constantly
All day, every day
Spoon-fed in brief
Digestible bits
Or, for the "free-thinker"
Who goes to social media
To huff and inject memes
Freshly made by Russians
To enrage and entertain
To echo the sentiments
Of the talking points
Marinating and washing
The smoothing folds
Of their brains

                November 19, 2024
                Lenox, Massachusetts

Written while listening to "Little Numbers" by BOY.

November

I Might Need Another Month

How can it be
Nearly the holidays
When the weather
Hasn't dipped
In the direction
It should be going
To make it feel like
It's time for the season
The lights are going up
The songs are playing now
The stores are pushing
All of their seasonal selling
But it still feels like
Early October
Not late November
So, I might need
Another month
To be created
And placed
Between this one
And December
To make time feel right

    November 19, 2024
    Lenox, Massachusetts

Written while listening to "Crystalised" by The xx.

At These Latitudes

This time of the year
Is when the sun
At these latitudes
Is more lackadaisical
Than in summer June
Getting up late
Not venturing
All that far
Instead choosing
Relative quietness by
Staying southerly
Before retiring
Hopping the horizon
For the night
By 4:30
Leaving all of us
To long for
The brighter
The longer
The warmer days
Of yore
When the day
Had so much more
Potential

        November 19, 2024
        Lenox, Massachusetts

Written while listening to "Old Town Blues" by Boy & Bear.

November

The Fruitless Effort

The fruitless effort
Of the current season
Is to seek and remove
Every goddamn leaf
From every inch
Of every yard
In the country
In the continued quest
For visual perfection
Despite the naturalist's pleas
To just please leave them be

        November 19, 2024
        Lenox, Massachusetts

Written while listening to "Viva l'amour" by Sabina Sciubba.

An Apology To The Birds

I want to get the bird feeder going
But At the same time
I'm a little nervous
That the local bear population
Hasn't yet gone to bed
For their seasonal slumber
So, for the moment
An apology to the birds
As I wait for it to get colder

        November 19, 2024
        Lenox, Massachusetts

Written while listening to "Running Back To You" by The Juan Maclean.

November

Play It Endlessly On Repeat

All of the people who are now
Coming out of the woodwork
With their shocked Pikachu faces
Crying, wailing, yelling, pleading
They had regrets and no idea
That he would do this or that
And never would have voted
For him if they had only known
And to all of these dummies
We can only cue up the line
"He said he was gonna"
And play it endlessly on repeat

>November 19, 2024
>Lenox, Massachusetts

Written while listening to "Sunspell" by Geotic.

A Pretty Great Idea

While the world I have known
Is overwhelmed and taken down
In the right-wing orgy of dismantling
Societal systems and checks and balances,
I can't help but long for and plan
My own exit from this stupid place
Somewhere where cooler heads prevail
Where improving society as a whole
Is something that is generally thought of
As a pretty great idea worth promoting

>   November 19, 2024
>   Lenox, Massachusetts

Written while listening to "Saturnine" by GoGo Penguin.

November

Fran Lebowitz

My wife asked me to buy tickets
To a speaking thing as Mass MoCA
She gave me the date and the time
And said it was for Fran Lebowitz
And I thought that it was weird
That the lady who takes pictures of babies
In flowerpots was going to speak
At a modern art museum, but whatever
When I said this to my wife
She was like "Not the flowerpot baby lady"
That's Anne Geddes
So, I then thought, OHHH!
This is that famous photographer woman
Thinking it was Annie Leibovitz
But once again
I was very wrong
But at least now
I have a few months
To learn all about Fran Lebowitz
Before we see her speak in March

                November 20, 2024
                Lenox, Massachusetts

Written while listening to "Such Great Heights" by The Postal Service.

The Lunch Void

I forgot to prepare
A nice nutritious lunch
Before leaving for work
So, in that case
This bag of tortilla chips
And this jar of salsa
Will fill the lunch void
Succinctly

                November 21, 2024
                Lenox, Massachusetts

Written while listening to "All My Heart" by STRABE.

November

Not Enough To Stop

The gentle rain
Falling through
The cold air
Is peaceful
But not enough
To make up for
The three months
With no rain
And not enough
To stop the fire
Burning through
A nearby town

        November 21, 2024
        Lenox, Massachusetts

Written while listening to "Grumpus (live)" by Lambchop.

Splitting Hairs

Splitting hairs
Regarding the
Definition of
The thing
They are
Dancing around
Trying not to
Make it seem
As horrible as
It really is
When in reality
It's much much worse

    November 21, 2024
    Lenox, Massachusetts

Written while listening to "Tearing Me Up" by Bob Moses.

Absorb It All

I crave a more
Art-filled existence
One populated completely
With color and beauty
One that makes
My eyes smile
At every turn
In every direction
In a width of styles
And a depth of breadth
Just art
Absolutely everywhere
My own or
Anyone else's
I don't care
Just get it here
And let me absorb it all

        November 21, 2024
        Lenox, Massachusetts

Written while listening to "Dance Yrself Clean" by MS MR.

The New Annual Norm

When "once-a-century" storms
Are now the new annual norm
We've somehow broken
The predictability of the planet
For convenience and profit

        November 21, 2024
        Lenox, Massachusetts

Written while listening to "Breathe Me - Milo remix" by Sia and Milo MacInnes.

November

Yet Another

Trying to shield
A sexual predator
And noted law breaker
So he can become
The nation's top cop
The Attorney General
Is yet another
Disgustingly despicable
Horrible example
Of the fucked-up direction
Our country is heading in

    November 21, 2024
    Lenox, Massachusetts

Written while listening to "Comatose" by Jobii.

High Art

Is a banana
Duct taped
To a wall
High art
Or possibly
A crude way
Of facilitating
Money laundering
Either way
The "piece" lacks
The "brilliance"
Used to describe it

        November 21, 2024
        Lenox, Massachusetts

Written while listening to "Star" by Jon Gurd.

November

I Have No Choice But To Risk It

This morning
I realized
With annoyance
That I left
My leftovers
From Thanksgiving
Out all night
Instead of putting them
In the fridge
So, I immediately went
To Google
To see if it was still safe
To eat
And pretty much everything
Said it wasn't worth the risk
And to just toss it
But
It was so delicious
And so expensive
That I feel like
I have no choice
But to risk it
And you will know
The outcome
If there is another poem
After this one

    November 29, 2024
    Lenox, Massachusetts

Written while listening to "Hours" by Tycho.

The Comfortable In-Between

DECEMBER

The Lightest Glaze

The lightest glaze
Of the powdered snow
Existing in the areas
Shielded by shadows
On the sunny days
With all other ground
Still greenish brown
With the snow-free grass

        December 3, 2024
        Lenox, Massachusetts

Written while listening to "Take My Hand" by Matt Berry.

December

The Stark Line

The stark line
In the backyard
Greenish grass
To the north
Only snow
To the south
Showing the place
Where the sun's
Heat ray lasers
Can't rise past
This northernly space
Past the roofline
Of my modest house

    December 3, 2024
    Lenox, Massachusetts

Written while listening to "Red Bull & Hennessy" By Jenny Lewis.

Coincidence

Coincidence
Leads to
Thinking
About the
Possibilities
And the
Outcomes
If this was done
Instead of the way
I was doing it
Before I realized
This new way
Was more
In line
With how I imagined
Things should be

                December 3, 2024
                Lenox, Massachusetts

Written while listening to "Trojans" by Atlas Genius.

December

Nothing Gets In The Way Of Profit

The healthcare company
Whose CEO was shot
Did not let this stop
The shareholder meeting
Which happened on time
While the CEO was dying
Showing that nothing
Gets in the way of profit

        December 6, 2024
        Lenox, Massachusetts

Written while listening to "The Sugar Troubles" by Sonorous Star.

Insulating

Health care companies
Are now busy insulating
Their top decision makers
From being known at all
To the general public
Removing them from
Their websites as a way
To protect them from us,
The people they deny
Life-saving procedures,
The people who die
Without the medicines
They refuse to pay for
With decisions made by
A computerized AI
Whose only deciding factor
Is how to maximize profit

    December 6, 2024
    Lenox, Massachusetts

Written while listening to "Katie Queen of Tennessee" by The Apache Relay.

December

The Light Fluffy Snow

The light fluffy snow
That fell the other day
Fun, pretty, and beautiful
Has had time to sit
And be exposed
To the bitter cold
Freezing the moisture
Making it crunchy
Hard, and rough –
Difficult to navigate
Making it a hazard
For anywhere not cleared

              December 6, 2024
              Lenox, Massachusetts

Written while listening to "Sonate Pacifique" by L'Imperatrice.

Lighting The Way

I think I just got
Something akin
To a kick in the pants
By The Universe
With my writing
And the direction
I want to be going
As the coincidences
Keep piling up
In an endless
Cosmic car crash
That makes each one
Impossible to ignore
Especially as they
Burst into flames
Lighting the way
For me to go

                December 6, 2024
                Lenox, Massachusetts

This is unrelated to my poetry writing.

Written while listening to "Falling Down The Stairs Of Your Smile" by The New Pornographers.

December

Four Tarot Cards

Last month
Our country
Drew four
Tarot cards
And they were
The ten of swords
The five of swords
The Five of cups
And The Tower
Which, when you
Combine them all
Basically turns into
A toilet card
Flushing us all
Down the drain

           December 6, 2024
           Lenox, Massachusetts

Written while listening to "You and I" by Washed Out.

Weekend Ahead

Weekend ahead
Beginning in just
A few minutes
Making me start
To pack up
To get ready
To get going
Home

                December 6, 2024
                Lee, Massachusetts

Written while listening to "Guggenheim" by The Ting Tings.

December

Chilly Stick Season

Watching the
Melting happen
In real time
As it gets
Warmer
And the grass
Becomes more
Visible
In patches
Between the bits
Of snow
Fading quickly
Along with the
Memories of the
Seasonal snowfall
We had last week
As we resume
With chilly stick season

        December 10, 2024
        Lenox, Massachusetts

Written while listening to "Breathe Me In" by STRABE.

While The Countries

While the countries
Who have the highest
Standard of living
Celebrate knowledge
And advancement
Of our collective humanity
While distributing
The Nobel prizes this week
Our country
Which used to be known
Among them at one point
Is gleefully preparing
The gluttonous gutting
Of our government's resources
As an all-you-can-eat buffet
For the billionaires among us
Stripping it all for parts
Ensuring that when they are gone
The rusted remains
Will be of use to no one

    December 10, 2024
    Lenox, Massachusetts

Written while listening to "Everyday Is Like Sunday" by Morrissey.

December

Sometimes The Weight

Sometimes the weight
Of this space
In the place
Just takes a toll
Like a roof
Covered in snow
Too deeply to hold
For much longer
Worries
Like flakes
Are tiny
And overlooked
Until they team up
Pile up
And press down
Making this
Combined weight
Clearly felt
To the point
Where
Continuing
Seems nearly
Impossible

    December 10, 2024
    Lenox, Massachusetts

Written while listening to "Lazuli" by Beach House.

Dark Day

Dark day
Full of rain
Warm for December
Vanishing all the snow
Leaving the confused grass
Who've been used to
A blanket of snow
But now their sleep
Has been interrupted
Three months early
In the wrong season
And the wrong year
Because the climate
Is getting confused
Along with the rest of us

    December 11, 2024
    Lenox, Massachusetts

Written while listening to "Pain" by The War On Drugs.

December

Drop Splashing

The rain falling
Sounding like
A wet sizzling
Rhythm hitting
The pavement
Drop splashing
In puddles pooling
Busy reflecting
The blotted gray above

        December 11, 2024
        Lenox, Massachusetts

Written while listening to "Personal Jesus" by Depeche Mode.

Doing The Best He Can

An old man
Barely able to walk
Difficulty trying to think
Gets in his car
And creeps along
He probably shouldn't be
Behind the wheel
But in this country
There is no choice
With no public transportation
And no way to get
Across towns so spread out
He's doing the best he can
Until the day comes
When he can't

    December 11, 2024
    Lenox, Massachusetts

Written while listening to "Dancing On My Own" by Jake McMullen.

December

Listening To What The Rain Was Saying

Where did the snow go?
It lay there listening
To what the rain was saying
The sweet nothings
Eventually convincing
The snow
To change their ways
Succumbing to the heat
Becoming more fluid
Until every last bit of white
Liquified and flowed freely
Into the ground
Off on a new adventure
Intertwined with the rain
And it's swaying ways

        December 11, 2024
        Lenox, Massachusetts

Written while listening to "It's All Downhill From Here" by Scout.

Late To Start

Late to start
With decorating
After a late
Thanksgiving
Making all the fuss
Seem not worth it
When it'll all
Have to come down
In a couple of weeks
So, why bother
Getting it all out
Spending hours
Putting it all up
Only to enjoy it
For so little time
Before returning
It all to the basement
Which is why
This year
We half-assed it
With decorating

                December 11, 2024
                Lenox, Massachusetts

Written while listening to "Oobleck" by Kaki King.

December

The Wondering

The wondering
About the past
Sometimes
Overtakes
The present
Like thinking about
The What Ifs
Which is a road
When going down
Benefits nobody
As you sacrifice
And exchange
Present moments
For dwelling on
Past potential scenarios

    December 12, 2024
    Lenox, Massachusetts

Written while listening to "Missing" by Everything But The Girl.

Writer's Block

There is no such thing
As writer's block
That all-defining malady
That's always stymieing
Writers the world over.
If you sit at a keyboard
The words will come
This little writing
Is proof of that
As when I looked
At this screen staring back
I had absolutely no idea
Of what I would write about
And then, the little voice
Casually mentioned
That I must have
Writer's block
Except I don't
And neither do you.

I can see
If you're trying
To force a script
Or a book to appear
When you're reeling
From a breakup,
Or a death, or something
Of the sort
That might be hard
But it's not writer's block
You've got too many other worries
That are more important
At the moment

Or, another possibility
Is that what you're trying
To create isn't interesting

December

Not even enough
To keep your own interest
To get it down on paper

In the end
If nothing comes
Take some time
Change your location
Put on some music
And try again

        December 12, 2024
        Lenox, Massachusetts

Written while listening to "Sweet Surrender" by Sarah McLachlan.

The Comfortable In-Between

Errant Flakes

The single errant flakes
Falling from the sky
Haven't a chance of a hope
Of making it for more
Than a few minutes
On a day like today
Where the sun's rays
Are converting the quarter inch
That fell during the night
Into water for the soil
But still
The brave snowflakes
Continue the mission
Of swirling in the wind
Falling and landing
Because that's what they do
Giving a sense of the season
When the weather
Isn't keen on cooperating

    December 12, 2024
    Lenox, Massachusetts

Written while listening to "West Coast" by Lana Del Rey.

December

Fight Or Flight

Thinking about 2025
And the upcoming year
Should I be afraid?
Should I start preparing?
Preparing for what?
To hunker down?
To defend my home?
Fight or flight?
Figuring out where
That would take me?
Planning for all
Possible contingencies?
Knowing some
Will never be touched
While others
Will be woefully not enough
But still should I try?

The answer to all of these
Is YES.

December 12, 2024
Lenox, Massachusetts

The Boy Scout Motto ("Be prepared") is hanging heavy in my head.

Written while listening to "Salta" by Sultan + Shepard.

Anger At The Buffet

The anger at the buffet
Feeds the needs
Of those wanting to eat
Their fears away
While blaming others
For each little thing

                December 12, 2024
                Lenox, Massachusetts

Written while listening to "The Wind" by PJ Harvey.

December

Trust The Intuition

Do I trust the intuition
Comforting me
Saying that
Everything will
Be okay and alright
Or do I listen instead
To my mind,
Busily fretting
And worrying
And planning
For things that
Haven't happened yet
And may never happen

                December 13, 2024
                Lenox, Massachusetts

Written while listening to "Chain Reaction" by Joy Downer.

Verbal Voyaging

Words are the means
The vehicle for
The emotions we feel
And just like getting
Behind the wheel
We need to be careful
With how we drive
Taking responsibility
For how we conduct
Our verbal voyaging

                December 13, 2024
                Lenox, Massachusetts

Written while listening to "Everything Is Alright" by Four Tet.

We Spend Both

Money equals time
In that we spend both
Although only one
Actually feels more real
And is measured by
The number in the bank
While the other is realer
With no measurement
Other than our aging
Because we never know
When we are running low
But, unlike cash in hand,
We can fit as much life
Into each day as we can

        December 13, 2024
        Lenox, Massachusetts

Written while listening to "Edge of Town" by Middle Kids.

The Comfortable In-Between

From Back In Simpler Times

Listening to a song
From back in simpler times
When the world seemed big
When our problems
Were being solved
When everything seemed
To be moving in the right direction
In the days when life
Seemed big and warm
And possibility was endless
When the color of hope
Was painted on everything
And the smell of potential
Was like fresh flowers in the air
And we were excited
To be here and be alive

December 13, 2024
Lenox, Massachusetts

Massively oversimplified and painted while wearing rose-tinted glasses, covered in rose petals, spritzed with rose-scented perfume by a woman named Rose.

Written while listening to "Return To Innocence" by Enigma.

December

Born This Week

Emily Dickinson's birthday
Was just the other day
And today belongs to
That person, the Tay-Tay,
Also known as Taylor Swift
Which makes me wonder
About something I had missed
Like a notice saying the founders
Of our poetic worldview
All had to be born this week

                December 13, 2024
                Lenox, Massachusetts

Written while listening to "Oracle" by Shikmo.

A Degree

They always say
"To a degree"
Meaning
Yes, to a point,
And implying
That you have
Not only reached
But exceeded
That point
In a way making
And marking
You as an idiot
But not overtly
Saying it so plainly

    December 17, 2024
    Lenox, Massachusetts

Written while listening to "Our Hearts Of Ruin" by Blue Sky Black Death.

December

Speedbumping

Dump out the smooth
Eschew the bland
Remove what lacks
The grittiness
The continued contrast
Speedbumping
Every second
Of the experience
Making you…
No, forcing you,
To face and accept
A worldview
That is completely new
To anything you have
Previously known

                December 17, 2024
                Lenox, Massachusetts

Written while listening to "Shoreline" by All Feels.

Tightrope Walking

Wanting a life
Different than this
While still appreciating
What I currently have
Is a bit like tightrope walking
Higher than I feel comfortable
Yes, I am here
Yes, I am happy
With what I have
But I still want more
In such a way
That would completely change
Nearly every aspect of my life
From place to work to home
To country to everything
All the while hoping
A gust of wind doesn't come along
And knock me down

    December 17, 2024
    Lenox, Massachusetts

Written while listening to "Love From The Other Side" by L'Imperatrice.

December

Vivid Remembrance

Me
Realizing
That I should be
Looking at
Everything
Through the eyes
Of someone who
Won't be seeing
Won't be experiencing
This location
Again
For a long time,
If ever,
Causing me
To appreciate
What I have now
In the moment
So that someday
I can look back
With more clarity
And vivid remembrance

    December 17, 2024
    Lenox, Massachusetts

Written while listening to "Maybe Tomorrow" by Pretty Lights.

Too Warm For December

A day
Too warm for December
More at home
In a month like October
But still
This is our world now
Where the non-seasonal days
Linger like a creeper
Leering and watching
As we relax in thinking
We can let down our guard
And then they leave
And sub-zero temperatures
Slam into the scene
Hitting harder
Stinging harsher
Than if we had just had
Seasonal days all along

    December 17, 2024
    Lenox, Massachusetts

Written while listening to "Sweet And Tender Hooligan" by The Smiths.

December

A Welcome Postcard

Window open
In mid-December
Seems wrong
But the day
Feels so right
The sun
And the warmth
Saying hello
A welcome postcard
From the last season
(Or, the next,)
That can be
Relived in this moment

           December 17, 2024
           Lenox, Massachusetts

Written while listening to "Alaska" by Maggie Rogers.

The Comfortable In-Between

With The Eagles Of My Future Self

Computer class
In middle school
Hands on keyboards
(Mice weren't a thing yet)
Causing a feeling
A knowing
That this is
The beginning
Of what will be
Something defining
In this current life
And then when in
Typing class
In high school
Hands on typewriters
Wanting to let my fingers
Go free and go flying
Over the keys
Felt like a moment
Where my soul self
Whispered to me
"Get ready"
While the gruff-voiced
Girls' soccer coach
Who doubled as
The typing teacher
Growled letters for us to type
"G-G-G-G-H-H-H-H"
Making me feel like
I was corralled with
Pre-school kids
When I should be
Boundlessly flying
With the eagles
Of my future self

December 17, 2024

December

Lenox, Massachusetts

Written while listening to "Whirring" by The Joy Formidable.

So Few Seconds

So many thoughts
So few seconds
Not enough time
To explore
Even a percent
Of what I find
Interesting and
Captivating
When I haven't
Even seen
A fraction
Of this wide
Wonderful world
And what I do see
Makes my thoughts
Bubble over
With possibility
That I know
Can also never
Ever be fully explored

     December 17, 2024
     Lenox, Massachusetts

Written while listening to "Bloom" by Kaizen and Shinigami.

December

My Heart Expects It

I do not write for you
I don't even write for me
I write because
My heart expects it
Like a type
Of journalistic therapy

December 17, 2024
Lenox, Massachusetts

Written while listening to "Would've, Could've, Should've" by Taylor Swift.

Coincidental note: It's April 20, 2025 and I'm editing this collection (so late! Sorry!) and I'm not even remotely kidding, but when my eyes landed on "Written while listening to…" that exact song started playing on my phone.

Unaware Of The Options

Unaware of the options
Available to me
When I was of the age
Where I should have been
Focusing on a direction
Instead of plodding along
Sort of in one way
But then wanting to change
And realizing too late
That trying to change
Is like hitting a reset button
With no experience
And no education
To back up the new thing
Making me fall
Through the cracks
Where I find myself now

    December 17, 2024
    Lenox, Massachusetts

Written while listening to "Gumball Machine Weekend" by Yppah.

December

Manufactured Escape

Lighter
Fluffier
The sweetly
Overly
Sickly
Candy
Coating
Covering
Everything
Where they
Are always
Keeping
It as bright
And light
As possible
While hiding
Anything
Resembling
Reality
With their
Manufactured
Escape

December 18, 2024
Lenox, Massachusetts

Written while listening to "Surfin" by Memory Cassette.

The Beats

The formula
We've been
Drinking
Since forever
Are the beats
That drive
The story
With no
Deviation
Possible
For anything
Hoping to
Get bought
Or made.

It's this
Or it's nothing.

    December 18, 2024
    Lenox, Massachusetts

I've got *Save The Cat* on my brain.

Written while listening to "Long Way Down" by Pete Yorn.

December

Delft

I just want to be
A beautiful thing
A Delft human
Or something fun
Like that
That can be
Appreciated
But at the same time
I want the ability
To change the manner
Of how I look
When the mood strikes
Because being
The same thing
Forever and ever
Is nothing I want
A part of at all

        December 18, 2024
        Lenox, Massachusetts

Written while listening to "Half Awake" by Porcelain Raft.

The Comfortable In-Between

Watching Out The Window

Watching out the window
While doing the things
I want to do
Keeping an eye out
For anyone incoming
So I can look busy
Is probably not
the best use of my time
But here I sit
And here I am
For my required hours
Each and every day

                December 18, 2024
                Lenox, Massachusetts

Written while listening to "Beesting" by Winterpills.

December

The Patterns Of The Clouds

The patterns of the clouds
Are entrancing
While the continual shifting
Of their moving
Is constantly changing
The view from second
To second
Making it all
So much more interesting

    December 18, 2024
    Lenox, Massachusetts

Written while listening to "Entangled" by Klur.

People Are Forgotten

The legacy one leaves behind
For most of us is instantly brief
Since the pandemic, funerals
Aren't really a thing anymore
Instead, it's a short outpouring
Of "aw shucks" and "too bad"
On their Facebook wall or on
Their preferred platform of choice
If they had children or grandchildren
They'll be remembered here and there
In a moment of reflection or memory
For a generation or two at the most
But after that, people are forgotten

                    December 18, 2024
                    Lenox, Massachusetts

Written while listening to "One Day They'll Know (ODESZA Remix)" by Pretty Lights.

December

Doubly Determined

To know
What you want
And not have it
Does two things
It makes you
Intensely sad
For existing
Without it
While also being
Doubly determined
To achieve it

                December 18, 2024
                Lenox, Massachusetts

Written while listening to "Midnight City" by M83.

A Casualty

Lacking awareness
Of your surroundings
Can lead to anger
From those who
Inhabit your vicinity
Or can lead to
An accident
Where someone
Ends up a casualty
Due to your stupidity

    December 18, 2024
    Lenox, Massachusetts

Written while listening to "Pacific State" by 808 State.

December

The Day After The Exchange Of Power

Uncertainty
Has officially
Gotten in the way
Of something
We wanted to do
Despite everything
Seeming normal
At the moment
But the date
Is the day after
The exchange power
And being in mid-town
New York City
Is the last place
We want to be

           December 19, 2024
           Lenox, Massachusetts

The Taskmaster Series 19 World Premiere is going to be done as a live event at The Town Hall venue in New York City on January 21, 2025. When I saw it on Instagram I went crazy instantly figuring out the logistics of getting to NYC on a Tuesday and spending the night there and returning on Wednesday…but then I saw the date and as much as I desperately wanted to go, my intuition was telling me to "hunker down" in case weird shit went down after he takes office again (especially since he said he would be a dictator on his first day). In the end, we discussed it and thought, just in case, we should sit this one out.

Written while listening to "Be A Rebel" by New Order.

The Comfortable In-Between

The Cultural Season

Inching closer
To the day
The reason
For the lights
We celebrate
The music
The decorations
The cards
The spending
The cultural season
We, in our country,
Participate in

        December 20, 2024
        Lenox, Massachusetts

When it's all said and done, I'll most miss the lights.

Written while listening to "Carol Of The Bells" by Ashnikko.

December

The Snow Is Here

The snow is here
This weekend
It won't be
As the temperature
Is sure to hide it
Where we will
No longer be
Able to see it

        December 27, 2024
        Lenox, Massachusetts

Written while listening to "Telephone" by Sinkane.

The Comfortable In-Between

Productivity Has Melted

Sitting alone
At work
On the Friday
Between the
Big holidays
When productivity
Has melted
To a new low
Ensuring that
Nothing really
Gets done
Other than
Preparing for
The weekend

                December 27, 2024
                Lenox, Massachusetts

Written while listening to "Whenever" by Hotlane.

December

The Near-Vicinity

Times when I have
Lived in the center
Of things going on
Have been very slim
But actually more
Like on the fringes
In the near-vicinity
Like being on the
Outskirts of a city
You can clearly see
The pretty lights from
At night when you
Sit and stare at the view

        December 27, 2024
        Lenox, Massachusetts

Written while listening to "Spectrum" by Max Cooper.

The Comfortable In-Between

The Ideas Never Stop

The ideas never stop
Despite me being so
Casual and careless
With them, having
Forgotten so many
Lost track of others
And messed up the
General idea of the rest
Yet, they still come
Like an endless wave
From some source
Far away in the distance

>December 27, 2024
>Lenox, Massachusetts

Written while listening to "Punk Rock Girl" by The Dead Milkmen.

December

Impossibly Stacked

While I believe
That the lottery
Is impossibly
Stacked against
Everyone who plays
Having over a billion
Reasons to buy a ticket
Is a pretty big thing
That's pretty hard to ignore

>December 27, 2024
>Lenox, Massachusetts

The Mega Millions lottery is over a billion dollars tonight.
(Note: I did not win.)

Written while listening to "Groove Is in the Heart" by Deee-Lite.

Threaten Greenland

What kind of blithering idiot
Thinks it's perfectly fine
And absolutely normal
To threaten Greenland
One of the quietest, nicest,
And backgroundy
Countries in all the world

                December 27, 2024
                Lenox, Massachusetts

Written while listening to "Red Lights" by Holy Fuck.

(Note: if I were choosing songs that specifically correlated with the poems I wrote, I would have been listening to "Shaft In Greenland" by The Dead Milkmen.)

December

Changing My Focus

While I know
That all of the chatter
Being focused on
In the present moment
Is very doom and gloom
(All for very good reasons)
I am now
Changing my focus
From outward to inward
Turning the volume down
On the useless, negative
Too-loud screaming
I am constantly hearing
And turning up
The volume on my own
Intuition and inner voice
Focusing on myself
My projects, and my art
(Visual and written)
Because I know
This will better serve me
For the years to come

    December 27, 2024
    Lenox, Massachusetts

Written while listening to "Montrose Ave" by Y.V.E. 48.

The Comfortable In-Between

The place we often
Just mean to pause
And take a rest in
Is where we ended up
Staying for years in
Is the comfortable
In-between –
The pausal couch
We can't get off of
Between where
We came from
And where we
Really want to be
The inadvertent
Rest stop that we
Forgot to set
An alarm at,
Telling us
To get up and
Get a move on
Overstaying
Our intended
Intermission
We've been here
Entirely too long
But it's too hard
To easily move
Getting up and
Moving forward
From this entirely
Comfortable and
Very pretty place

December 28, 2024
Lenox, Massachusetts

December

A recent realization.

Written while listening to "Thinning" by Snail Mail.

The Comfortable In-Between

Only A Few Hours Left

Approaching the end
Of the year
Only a few hours left
Even though
It's the same life
The division between
Years is a stark reminder
That everything
Begins and ends
And that our time
Is incredibly limited
Despite that, in a few days
I'll be starting the next
Poetry collection
As I normally do
But this one here
Will be stuck firmly
In the past
Back in 2024
Which is now over
Its potential
Fully used up
With nothing
Remaining
Other than memories
As we move on
Into a new year
With new hopes
And new fears

December 31, 2024
Lenox, Massachusetts

Written while listening to "Nice Weather for Ducks" by Lemon Jelly.

December

IF YOU ENJOYED THIS COLLECTION

Please consider rating it at Amazon.com. As an independent author, having people review my works is critical in helping to increase my exposure and letting new people discover books like this. Thank you!

The Comfortable In-Between

WRITTEN BY ERIC NIXON

The Comfortable In-Between – 2024 poetry collection
When Time Was Stable – 2023 poetry collection
Indestructible – 2022 poetry collection
The Length Of A Second – 2021 poetry collection
The Year That Aged Us – 2020 poetry collection
You Are A Poet – guided poetry journal
Caught In Pause – 2019 poetry collection
Equidistant – 2018 poetry collection
The Cupcake – 2017 poetry collection
2492: Attack Of The Ancient Cyborg – science fiction novel
The Ocean Above – 2016 poetry collection
Cascadia's Fault – 2015 poetry collection
The Taborist – 2014 poetry collection
The Entire Universe – 2013 poetry collection
Trying Not To Blink – 2012 poetry collection
Lost In Thought – poetry collection
Emily Dickinson – Superhero: Vol. 1 – historical fiction novel
Incident On The Hennepin – a short story set in *2492*
Plenty Of Time – a short story
Retribution On A Jetpack – a short story set in *2492*
Anything But Dreams – poetry collection

Available at Amazon.com/author/ericnixon

ABOUT THE AUTHOR

Eric Nixon is a poet and author who has written fifteen poetry collections, a guided poetry journal, several short stories, and two novels – *2492: Attack Of The Ancient Cyborg* and *Emily Dickinson, Superhero: Vol. 1*. Eric lives in the Berkshires of western Massachusetts with his author wife, Kari Chapin Nixon.

www.ingramcontent.com/pod-product-compliance
Lightning Source LLC
Chambersburg PA
CBHW071646090426
42738CB00009B/1435